REALITY CHECK

REALITY CHECK

*The Unreported Good News
About America*

Dennis Keegan & David West

"Facts are stubborn things; and whatever may be our wishes, our inclinations, or the dictates of our passion, they cannot alter the state of facts and evidence."

—*President John Adams*

Cataloging-in-Publication data on file with the Library of Congress
ISBN 978-1-59698-560-5

Published in the United States by
Regnery Publishing, Inc.
One Massachusetts Avenue, NW
Washington, DC 20001
www.regnery.com

Manufactured in the United States of America

10 9 8 7 6 5 4 3 2 1

Books are available in quantity for promotional or premium use. Write to Director of Special Sales, Regnery Publishing, Inc., One Massachusetts Avenue NW, Washington, DC 20001, for information on discounts and terms or call (202) 216-0600.

Contents

About the Authors

Dennis Keegan is Chairman and Chief Investment Officer of the Auspex Group, a hedge fund headquartered in Greenwich, Connecticut. Previously, he served for fifteen years with Salomon Brothers, Inc., in New York and London. During his career with Salomon Brothers he headed U.S. proprietary trading, European fixed income arbitrage, and foreign exchange. He was chairman of Salomon's risk management committee, co-head of global fixed income, and co-chief executive of European operations. Mr. Keegan earned has bachelor's degree in economics at UCLA, and an MBA from the Anderson School of Business at UCLA. He currently serves on the Anderson School's Board of Visitors.

David W. West is Founder and CEO of Civicom, an advanced telecom and web-conferencing services company. He is former general manager of a division of Nestlé, the world's largest food company, where he championed a number of highly successful new businesses. He earned an MBA from Harvard Business School, where he also received a "Making a Difference" Award for his pioneering work in corporate philanthropy.

Introduction

PERCEPTION VERSUS REALITY

Any American who travels internationally gains a perspective of the United States that is often quite different from that provided by the prevailing news and politics back home. Returning from a third world country where the average income is less than $6,000 a year, with millions living on as little as $3.00 a day, where corruption and fraud are widespread, where unemployment is 8% or higher, where utilities and simple services we take for granted in this country don't work, and where health standards are low, you might find it hard to appreciate the constant blather about polls indicating how disappointed Americans are with the condition of the country. You might be a little less tolerant of the complaints of politicians and pundits about how "broken" our government is. While there are certainly things we'd all like to improve, America is still the standard by which the rest of the world defines success.

If, while engaged in a conversation about the state of the country with a recent American college graduate, you said that huge tax cuts for the rich and outrageous spending on two wars was bankrupting the U.S. economy, he would probably agree with you. He has been told that the U.S. economy is a disaster for six years now. He believes the war in Iraq was justified solely by falsehoods and probably thinks the endeavor is doomed. He is convinced that American "go it alone diplomacy" has isolated the U.S. and increased the risk of nuclear disaster. He's heard endlessly that FEMA's poor response to hurricane Katrina demonstrated the incompetence and the apathy of the U.S. government. In fact, you could say almost anything negative about the US and he would say, "Right . . . tell me something I didn't know."

The problem is, not one of these notions—which have in many circles become the generally accepted conventional wisdom—is true. Since, as we all know, "you're entitled to your own opinion, but not your own facts," this book is going to provide the ignored facts concerning these and other important issues where misconceptions exist.

We can not cover every important current issue, so we've chosen those where we felt the biggest gap exists between perception and reality. For example:

- The economy has not been a disaster. In fact, America's real growth rate over the past six years ranks near the top of developed nations.
- Tax cuts and military spending have not caused unprecedented budget deficits. In fact, the deficit is lower as a percent of Gross Domestic Product (GDP) than it was during the '90s, '80s, and '70s. And defense spending has been lower as a percent of GDP than it was fifteen years ago when there were no major conflicts.
- "Tax cuts for the rich" have not led to a huge increase in income disparity. In fact, the top income earners are paying a higher percentage of taxes today than ever before. Tax revenues are a higher percent of GDP than they were seven years ago.
- The Bush administration hasn't had a failed "go-it-alone" foreign policy that endangered the U.S. In fact, U.S.-led coalitions in Iraq and Afghanistan were significantly larger than for the first Gulf War. Of the five nations that posed a nuclear threat when President Bush took office, three (Iraq, Libya, and Syria)

have been eliminated and another (North Korea) appears to be on the verge of elimination, as a result of multilateral pressure and strength.*

If you find these facts surprising, it means there really is a perception/reality gap on these important issues. There are many more to come in this book.

WHY SHOULD YOU CARE?

When falsehoods prevail, bad decisions follow. It's hard enough to make good decisions on complex issues even when starting out with solid information. But if you start with bad information and wrong decisions, unintended consequences will almost certainly be the result. One of the most successful business leaders of our time, Jack Welch, had a well publicized set of rules that guided his decisions. The first was:

"Face reality as it is, not as you wish it were."
—*Jack Welch, former CEO of General Electric*

---

*Countries currently engaged in supporting U.S. effort in Iraq include Afghanistan, Albania, Angola, Australia, Azerbaijan, Bulgaria, Colombia, Czech Republic, Denmark, Dominican, Republic, El Salvador, Eritrea, Estonia, Ethiopia, Georgia, Honduras, Hungary, Iceland, Italy, Japan, Kuwait, Latvia, Lithuania, Macedonia, Marshall Islands, Micronesia, Mongolia, Netherlands, Nicaragua, Palau, Panama, Philippines, Poland, Portugal, Romania, Rwanda, Singapore, Slovakia, Solomon Islands, South Korea, Spain, Tonga, Turkey, Uganda, Ukraine, the United Kingdom, the United States, and Uzbekistan, and the number is still growing. The list includes nations from every continent. Population of coalition countries totals more than 1.23 billion people, with a combined GDP of approximately $22 trillion and represents every major race, religion, and ethnicity. It should come as no surprise that many of these countries have recently overthrown repressive regimes or have suffered from terrorist activities. These 49 nations understand the threat that Saddam Hussein posed to the world and the devastation his regime inflicted on their own people.

This was Jack's *most important* rule because wishful thinking and selective perception can influence judgment—and affect decisions—powerfully. Most people tend to hear what is emotionally expedient. We gravitate toward what reinforces our belief system and, therefore, won't require the difficult task of rearranging memory chunks and thought patterns. If people consistently select only those sources of information that comfortably fit their biases, false conclusions and bad decisions naturally follow. When the future of a country is at stake, we of course all want to avoid bad decisions.

WHY THIS BOOK IS NEEDED: PART 1—MEDIA CHAOS

It's no longer news to say that the mass media is undergoing a major transition. This book is not about the media, but it is worth reviewing the key events that have changed the character of the news we get from the media. They include:

1. TV news fragmentation elevated competition.
2. Increased amounts of unfiltered, unchecked information became available through the Internet.
3. Classified ad alternatives like eBay, AutoTrader.com, Monster.com and Craigslist took revenue from traditional media.
4. Two very close and contentious presidential elections increased partisan rhetoric.
5. A controversial war in Iraq raised the emotional vitriol.

One might have expected that the dramatic increase in the amount of information available and its frictionless transfer would have led to more reliable and accurate news. It seems the opposite has actually happened. Not too long ago, we had a choice of three mono-lithic evening news programs, run by editors and producers who made their best effort to adhere to conventional standards of "journalistic ethics"—reporting unbiased information. These three news machines and their print periodical counterparts were supported by armies of reporters and analysts who literally covered the globe.

Today the news is delivered 24 hours a day by many networks and cable stations, and anyone with a camera and a broadband Internet connection can deliver their own version of the news to a digital world. Increased competition and today's fragmented audience makes it harder to support large news staffs. Of equal importance, online goods and service exchanges like Craigslist, eBay, Monster.com, AutoTrader.com, and countless others have stripped the newspapers of classified ad revenue, which by some accounts represented as much as two-thirds of their total income, and went a long way toward supporting their core news functions and the necessary analysis on information.

With more competition from all sides, and declining circulations/viewership and ad revenue, ratings pressure has pushed media outlets toward focusing on a particular market segment and a product designed to appeal to that segment—usually either liberal or conservative so that they can count on tuning in to their program. With more and more information careening through the newsrooms and less staff to fully evaluate its authenticity, the temptation to publish information that may or may not be true—but which reinforces its organizational bias—is stronger than ever. The result? Less information and more opinion—opinion designed to maximize entertainment value—which often means it's *biased for effect* behind either a liberal or conservative agenda. This, of course, is the opposite of journalistic integrity.

One result is a blurred line between fact and opinion. Even worse is the fact that if each outlet moves to either a liberal or conservative slant, one never knows whether information received is objective truth or just part of a narrative the outlet has chosen. Even on a talk show where both sides are represented, opinions are plentiful but facts are scarce. The importance of objectivity has been overtaken by the need to supply a narrative that gets a reaction or creates a "buzz." Critical thinking and skepticism are more important than ever. We must do our own homework to find the truth.

WHY THIS BOOK IS NEEDED: PART 2—MEDIA BIAS

The liberal bias of the media is nothing new. The facts on this subject could fill a book. Here are just a few:

- Five times more national journalists identify themselves as "liberal" (34%) than "conservative" (just 7%). By contrast the general public identifies itself as more conservative (33%) than liberal (20%).[1]
- In the nation's capital, reporters and editors are 12 times more likely to vote for a Democrat than a Republican.[2] The general public is of course about 50/50.
- Democrats get more coverage than Republicans (49% of news stories for Democrats versus 31% for Republicans).[3] And the "tone" of the coverage was more positive for Democrats (35% to 26%) than for Republicans.[4]

This whole area of debate was recently alluded to in an amusing column by *Wall Street Journal* columnist Peggy Noonan. In one of her more memorable columns, the former White House staffer said it's refreshing that journalists and broadcasters no longer pretend to be objective reporters. She writes:

Charging the news media with liberal bias is like charging the rain with being wet. It is of their essence, it is what they are. And pretending this is not so is a dull and stupid game. It's also over. It is a fiction that has been overtaken by events. In the new, more competitive era, with scores of stations competing for viewers, with everyone looking not for a broad base but a solid niche, it's foolish to force highly opinionated reporters to act as if they don't have opinions. After all, it's not as if they are fooling the audience. It would be more practical, and probably better and less infuriating for everyone, if all the TV news shows and networks would admit the truth, declare one's bias.

But therein lay the problem. If every reporter declared his or her bias, it might help, but they all claim to be unbiased. In a 2001 C-SPAN interview, former NBC News anchor Tom Brokaw insisted, "The idea that we would set out, consciously or unconsciously, to put some kind of an ideological framework over what we're doing is nonsense." Whatever Tom Brokaw says, the typical viewer of the news no longer believes the presentation will be objective. A 2004 Gallup poll examining public attitudes about the credibility of the news media found that 48% of Americans view the media as "too liberal" while just 15% view it as "too conservative." Roughly a third says the media's slant is "about right." The repetition of the same narrow version of the global events has killed the standards of carefully considered analysis. With such low expectations it is not surprising many viewers now gravitate toward those sources that deliver news and opinion that supports their own point of view.

So news fragmentation and extreme partisan divide fed the new world of blogs, email tirades, talk radio rants, and YouTube sarcasm. In this world, anonymous opinions ricochet off others' bluster without anyone considering that their ardent positions might be founded on quicksand. People stopped listening. Facts and critical thinking were left in the dust behind an information overload juggernaut. Objectivity has been lost, standards have been compromised in order to lower costs, and buzz has become more important than credibility. Chaos and confusion now reign.

Media organizations could have stepped into the breach and added value by doing the hard work of sorting through the morass and delivering unbiased truth. Instead, most took the easy route. They tried to exploit the public's confusion by advancing their own ideological biases in a misguided attempt to increase ratings by "giving the people what they want." In doing so, most of these media outlets have diminished their value, undervalued the intellect of the average American and driven most of us to look for other alternatives.

Thus, this book.

CRITICAL THINKING

An important lesson in critical thinking is that whenever we see information designed to imply that a trend is either good or bad, we ought to ask the question: *Compared to what?* There is a tacit implication that if something is up or down compared to what it was before, then it must be really good or really bad. But that's not always the case.

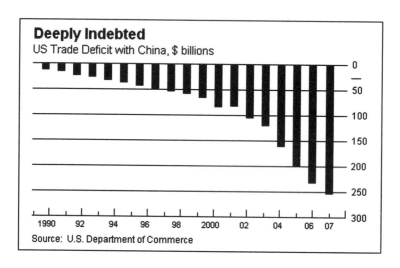

Deeply Indebted
US Trade Deficit with China, $ billions

Source: U.S. Department of Commerce

Here is a good example: A chart published in *The Economist* in 2008 shows a skyrocketing U.S. trade deficit with China. The U.S. is importing more goods from China than we export to China, and the chart shows this fact on a rapidly increasing basis. The chart makes the situation look dire. The average person seeing this chart would naturally assume that the nation is facing financial disaster, and our leaders are steering us toward imminent economic doom. They would believe America is exporting all of its jobs, and Americans will be working for the Chinese in no time at all. But is that really true? Most people have no idea whether a $250 billion trade deficit is significant in the context of the overall U.S. economy.

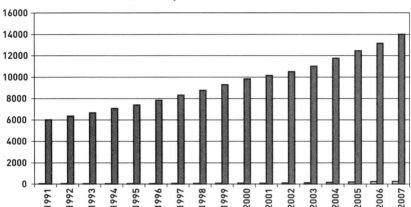

So let's ask: *Compared to what?* The chart below shows how this trade deficit with China looks in comparison to U.S. Gross Domestic Product over the same period.

It's the same information, but with some perspective. The trade deficit with China increased from 1% of U.S. GDP ($39 billion) in 1991 to 2% of GDP ($250 billion) in 2007, an increase of $211 billion. Meanwhile, the U.S. economy grew by $8 trillion. The economy's growth of $8 trillion is 38 *times* the deficit increase of $211 billion. Whether the increasing deficit with China is a good thing or a bad thing for America can be debated, but it's not in itself cause for alarm. It is, however, undoubtedly a big deal for China, where $250 billion represents more than 11% of the nation's GDP.

For another lesson in critical thinking—about how public opinion polls can mislead, through non-neutral language and biased sequencing of questions—see the afterword at the end of the book.

SETTING THE RECORD STRAIGHT

This book is not written as a defense of the White House or as an attack of any particular group. We have, however, chosen issues where the perception/reality gap seems greatest, and where providing a corrective assessment will be most useful and interesting. Given that news fragmentation and controversy increased dramatically since George Bush took office and the start of the war in Iraq, it should come as no surprise that we often benchmark trends from the start of the Bush administration. It should also come as no surprise that much of what we have to say is positive, because the media, by definition, tends to focus on the negative. At any moment, the story about a house that burned is more interesting than a story about the houses that didn't burn. Every once in a while, though, it's good to get away from the drumbeat of bad news and look at the big picture in perspective.

In each chapter we've followed a simple pattern, offering conventional wisdom, typical headlines or quotes from the media, followed by the facts, and our own analysis and opinions on the issues. Our plan has been to keep the opinions brief so that the salient material in each chapter will be the facts themselves, setting the record straight. For example, a section might begin with the conventional wisdom that China is about to overtake the United States economically, but that's not true. As the figures in this book will attest, China's economy is a fraction of our own, and while the so-called "Asian Tigers" are growing rapidly, it will be a long time before China or any of the other economies in the Far East come close to the size and affluence of the American economy.

We've done our own research. Everything we're presenting in these pages is readily available from sources anyone can examine. The problem is that most journalists aren't going to those sources. Most of the time it would appear they are reporting from the talking points of like-minded colleagues who represent a narrow range of opinion. A lot of people have misconceptions about which issues are most important to America's future. Where do they get these ideas? They get them from friends, from teachers, from others in the media, and many other places. But bad information leads to wrong choices, and our goal is to help remedy that situation.

AN INTERACTIVE PROCESS

For those who would like to comment or to provide additional input, we invite you to visit our website, *www.realitycheck-us.com*, where you will find portions of this text along with updated facts and commentary, more charts and graphs, and a page where you can add your own thoughts. Responsible debate is a good thing, but it's impossible to make rational choices without solid and reliable facts. That's what this work is all about. Thanks for coming with us on the journey.

Visit us at www.realitycheck-us.com

I

The Economy

1

An Economic Champion

CONVENTIONAL WISDOM

The economy has been in bad shape for years. Polls indicating that Americans are unhappy with the economy have emanated from the press for the last six years like a steady drumbeat.

Typical Headlines

"America's Economic Mood: Gloomy"
—*Wall Street Journal, Aug. 2, 2007*

"Bush's Legacy: Stagnant Pay and the Lowest Rate of Job Creation in the Last 40 Years"
—*Huffington Post, July 26, 2007*

Facts

America's real growth rate over the past five years ranks fourth among the 15 countries on *The Economist*'s list of developed nations. Two of the countries ahead of the U.S.—Australia and Sweden—are large commodity exporters and benefited from significant growth through price increases.

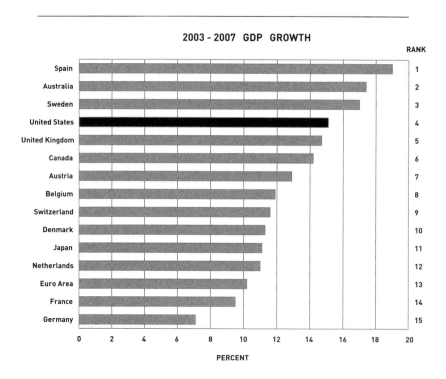

2003 - 2007 GDP GROWTH

	RANK
Spain	1
Australia	2
Sweden	3
United States	4
United Kingdom	5
Canada	6
Austria	7
Belgium	8
Switzerland	9
Denmark	10
Japan	11
Netherlands	12
Euro Area	13
France	14
Germany	15

PERCENT

Additionally

- **Unemployment** has been very low—a little above half that of most European countries—for years.
- **New job creation** has been strong. In November, 2007 a new record was set for the longest string of uninterrupted job growth months in U.S. history.
- **Productivity growth** has averaged 20% higher than Europe.*

The U.S. economy performed well or extremely well on all the most important measures from 2002 through 2007. Low unemployment and

---

* OECD Compendium of Productivity indicators 2005 Gap in GDP per hour worked (p. 27).

new job creations are important for obvious reasons. However, growth of the nation's Gross Domestic Product is generally considered the most important measure of economic health, because in the long run it correlates almost perfectly with prosperity.

WHAT IS GROSS DOMESTIC PRODUCT?

Gross Domestic Product (GDP) is simply the total value of all goods and services produced in the nation's economy. It is by far the most common measure of a country's economic growth. This is because it captures value created in a nutshell, and over the long run the material standard-of-living correlates closely with the value of goods and services that a society produces.

Gross Domestic Product is the most important measure of an economy, and real (inflation adjusted) long-term growth in GDP is the clearest signal of strength. For individuals to improve their income and wealth over time, the whole community must be producing and earning more. As productivity and profitability increase overall, income and wealth increase for individuals as well.

In most countries, the real increase in GDP generally comes from two sources: population growth and productivity growth. However, if GDP increases with population growth alone, the nation may be getting richer while the average citizen is maintaining essentially the same level of income and wealth. This means that GDP growth must exceed population growth for individuals to sustain an increase in their own incomes.

For a country to maintain total product growth above population growth, the productivity of each hour worked must increase. When this happens, employers can afford to pay more for that hour of work. The increased value added, then, generally comes from one of three sources:

- **Innovation:** An idea that takes the same amount of labor and makes a better product is key to significant improvement. An obvious example of innovation is computer power where, for example, a single Microsoft Excel spreadsheet can produce, in a moment, the work that would have required hours of clerical manpower twenty years ago.

- **Capital Investment:** The second major source of productivity growth involves an investment of both physical and mental resources. One man with proper training and skill in the use of an agricultural harvester can manage thousands of acres of farmland, producing many tons of grain. Fifty years ago, the same task would have required dozens of farmers and hundreds of laborers, to produce many fewer bushels of grain.

- **Comparative Advantage:** What comparative advantage means is that two countries by reallocating work between them can, in aggregate, produce more goods with less labor, meaning a greater level of productivity.

    A good example of this would be a situation in which the U.S. focuses more labor on making Boeing aircraft and Caterpillar tractors to sell to China. China, in turn, makes more Power Ranger and Star Trek action figures. The U.S., with a higher level of education and capital resources, makes investment-intensive goods, while China, with less investment in intellectual and physical capital, makes products that are generally more labor-intensive but less-intellectually intensive. This is, in fact, what's actually happening today.

Assessment

While soft spots exist in any economy, one can not suggest with intellectual integrity that the U.S. economy was a disaster under the Bush administration. In fact, the truth is just the opposite. Since informing the public about the economy is an important part of the press's responsibility, repeatedly broadcasting polls about Americans' disappointment with the economy amounts to publishing their own failing report card.

Yes, in early 2008 the combination of credit issues related to a real-estate bubble and crippling oil shock did finally manage to slow the strong economy. The other criticism is that real wage growth has not kept pace with GDP growth. This is true to some extent, but real wages have grown, and the growth rate will catch up over the long-run: it *always* does in free enterprise systems.

For most people a low unemployment trumps real wage growth. If you doubt that, you may want to contact someone in Germany or France and ask whether they would prefer their economy or ours. Unemployment in the Euro Zone countries, however, averaged 60% higher than the U.S. household unemployment rate from 2001 to 2007.

The individual years provide a time-lapse lesson in economic stimulus policy. In 2002, the year after the Bush administration cut tax rates, the U.S. grew 1.5%, which placed it in the top third of the pack in a year that the U.S. was recovering from the September 11 induced recession. In 2003, U.S. growth increased to 2.5%, making it fourth on the list of fifteen. This is no small achievement, as it is generally harder for large things to grow by a certain percentage than small things.[1]

In 2004, the U.S. economy grew by 3.6%. Some may remember hearing the mantra from some of the political candidates during that election year: This is the "worst economy since Herbert Hoover." If you put that in quotes and Google the phrase, you'll get more than 1,300 results. But, once again, that sort of rhetoric is so far from the facts it's almost laughable.

Take a look at the charts on these pages. The press was reporting on polls saying that the American people are dissatisfied with the economy, so when candidates repeated the same doom and gloom scenario over and over, somehow it seemed to be true. Yet, the fact is, the economy is strong and getting stronger. If the average person doesn't see the danger in this sort of perception/reality gap, at least they ought to see the risks involved in allowing misleading information to influence our thinking, and ultimately to influence national policy.

REALITY CHECK

2002 - GDP GROWTH

RANK

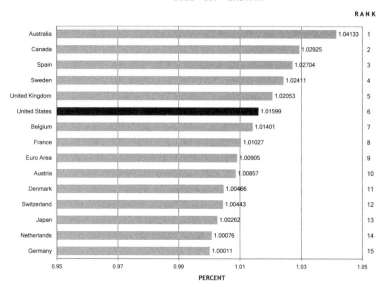

Country	Value	Rank
Australia	1.04133	1
Canada	1.02925	2
Spain	1.02704	3
Sweden	1.02411	4
United Kingdom	1.02053	5
United States	1.01599	6
Belgium	1.01401	7
France	1.01027	8
Euro Area	1.00905	9
Austria	1.00857	10
Denmark	1.00466	11
Switzerland	1.00443	12
Japan	1.00262	13
Netherlands	1.00076	14
Germany	1.00011	15

PERCENT

2003 - GDP GROWTH

RANK

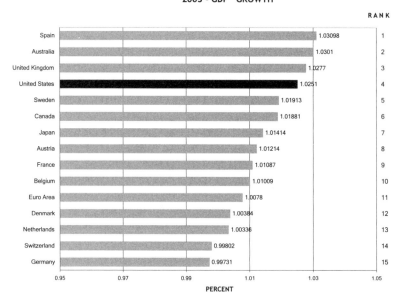

Country	Value	Rank
Spain	1.03098	1
Australia	1.0301	2
United Kingdom	1.0277	3
United States	1.0251	4
Sweden	1.01913	5
Canada	1.01881	6
Japan	1.01414	7
Austria	1.01214	8
France	1.01087	9
Belgium	1.01009	10
Euro Area	1.0078	11
Denmark	1.00384	12
Netherlands	1.00336	13
Switzerland	0.99802	14
Germany	0.99731	15

PERCENT

2004 - GDP GROWTH

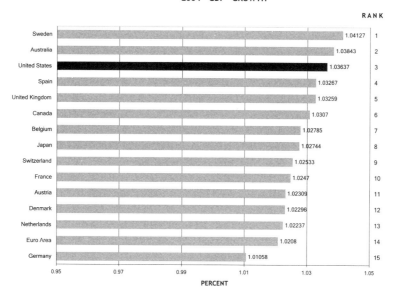

RANK

Country	Value	Rank
Sweden	1.04127	1
Australia	1.03843	2
United States	1.03637	3
Spain	1.03267	4
United Kingdom	1.03259	5
Canada	1.0307	6
Belgium	1.02785	7
Japan	1.02744	8
Switzerland	1.02533	9
France	1.0247	10
Austria	1.02309	11
Denmark	1.02296	12
Netherlands	1.02237	13
Euro Area	1.0208	14
Germany	1.01058	15

PERCENT

2005 - GDP GROWTH

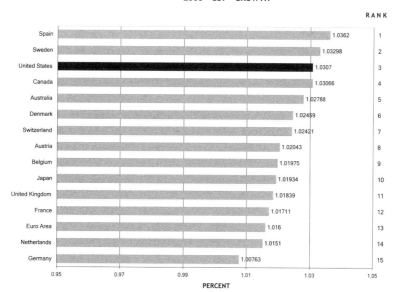

RANK

Country	Value	Rank
Spain	1.0362	1
Sweden	1.03298	2
United States	1.0307	3
Canada	1.03066	4
Australia	1.02788	5
Denmark	1.02459	6
Switzerland	1.02421	7
Austria	1.02043	8
Belgium	1.01975	9
Japan	1.01934	10
United Kingdom	1.01839	11
France	1.01711	12
Euro Area	1.016	13
Netherlands	1.0151	14
Germany	1.00763	15

PERCENT

In 2005, United States growth was ahead of all but one country on the list, with a growth of 3.1%. This is certainly not an economic disaster by any standard. There were years in the 1990s when the U.S. economy grew faster, but in those years America had more help driving the growth from other big economies.

As the charts on these pages show, the U.S. economy has experienced Real GDP growth in the range of 3% to 3.5% for several years. So is 3.5% a good rate of growth? Think of it this way: If we start with 100, grow by 3.5% to 103.5, then another 3.5% to 107.1, and do this five times, the economy will be 19% bigger than when it started. If the population grows by 1% per year, or 5% over five years, then real per capita growth will have grown by 14%. That's how America and individual Americans become wealthier.

STANDARDS FOR MEASURING GROWTH

Since there are several developing countries that have a faster growth rate than the ones shown in these charts, we need to take a moment to explain how the countries on this list were chosen. The financial publication, *The Economist,* has for many years published economic statistics for two groups of countries—developed countries and emerging countries. The list shown here is the complete list of developed countries for which a year to year comparison is shown.

Comparing the growth rates of developing economies like, for example, India or Singapore, each of which grew 8% in 2007, but are a small fraction (8% and 1% respectively) of the size of the U.S. economy, would not give useful comparisons. These countries are able to grow faster because they are, for the first time, becoming a part of world trade. Thus they are able to grow more rapidly because they are simply allocating their resources more efficiently than before, and they are able to borrow on the technology and business process innovations of the developed countries that have paved the way for

2006 - GDP   GROWTH

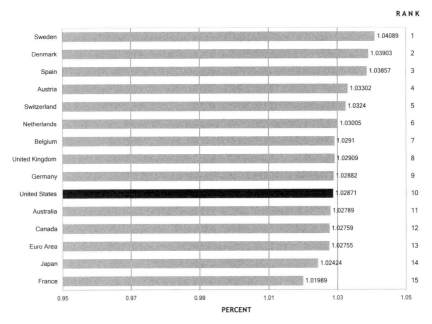

2007 - GDP   GROWTH

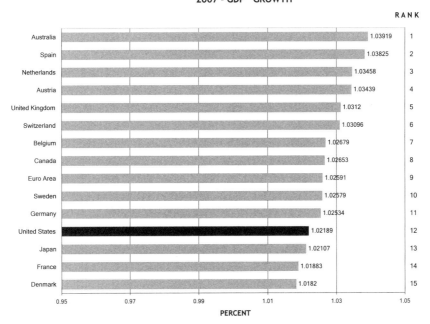

them. We're quick to say, however, that China is a special case, and we will deal with that country's remarkable growth in more detail in chapter 3.

In 2006 and 2007, the U.S. economy grew at 2.9% and 2.2%. These were healthy growth rates, but some European countries moved ahead of the U.S. So why were these countries suddenly doing so well? The answer: tax cuts throughout much of Europe spurred new growth.

CONVENTIONAL WISDOM

Economic decline has accelerated as a result of failed economic policies.

A Critical Assessment

The End of Affluence: The Causes and Consequences of America's Economic Decline, by Jeffrey Madrick offers a stark view of America's future. In this 1995 book, the author says American productivity is in irreversible decline, and he predicts that disputes over affirmative action, immigration, welfare reform, Social Security, environmental policy, and health care will lead to social chaos.

Facts

However the U.S.'s share of global GDP is higher today than twelve years ago. After declining from an estimated level of 75% of the world's GDP at the end of the Second World War to 25.1% in 1995, it—amazingly—increased to over 27% in 2006. Developing economies increased from 21.7% to 28.9%. The biggest share losers were Japan, France, and Italy.[2]

The U.S. is also ranked number one in competitiveness by the World Economic Forum, a Switzerland based think tank that grades 131 countries in 12 categories, including the quality of institutions, infrastructure, innovation, and macroeconomic stability. America's number one ranking is due, they said, to innovative companies, efficient capital markets, and a flexible workforce.

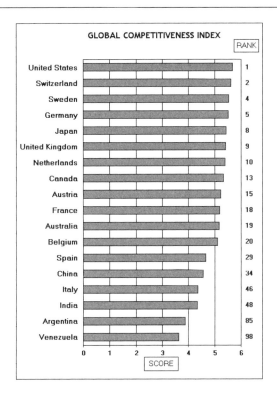

Assessment: When Perception Becomes Reality

One thing that politics and the financial markets have in common is that "the perception of reality" tends to become reality. In 1996, Alan Greenspan, then chairman of the Federal Reserve Bank and the nominal guardian of the U.S. banking system, said in a speech on central banking that the equity markets were "irrationally exuberant" and had separated themselves from reality.

Despite that observation, the markets continued even higher for nearly five more years before eventually dropping. Literally hundreds of billions of dollars were made by those who stayed "irrationally exuberant" until the third quarter of 2001. In 2002, under intense pressure from current events and other factors, the market finally collapsed.

When Greenspan made those remarks in 1996, the NASDAQ index of stocks was at 880. In 1999 the NASDAQ had traded as high as 4700, which was a gain of 430%. The momentum was strong, and perception was reality. By October 2001, the NASDAQ was trading down, at 790, a five year drop of 10%. The market psychology was based largely on hype, however, it remained real and very strong for a while. But eventually the reality shifted, and the facts had to rule.

In politics, if enough people believe in a politician or a political theory they can make that belief a reality by putting those people or ideas into positions of power. Whether that belief gives you Adolf Hitler, Soviet-style communism, or Richard Nixon does effect the reality. But if the facts are that the perception is wrong, the reality they've created will eventually adjust to truth. In that case, a dictator like Adolf Hitler will self destruct, communism will fall on its own sword of economic inadequacy, and Richard Nixon's inability to play by the rules will eventually destroy him.

In early 2008, Bear Stearns, an investment bank that had been around since 1923, was put out of business by fear of what might happen. Jimmy Cayne, the company's chairman, saw his $1 billion of stock fall to a value of $20 million. Alan Schwarz, who had become president in 2007, watched his company simply disappear. What happened was a typical "run on the bank." Banks and investment banks have hundreds of billions in securities on their balance sheets that are funded on a day-to-day basis. They are secure but highly leveraged entities. Even with plenty of equity, careful risk controls, and a solid record of profitable business dealings, the day the bank can't finance their daily position in securities markets is the day they are effectively out of business.

I know that personally. In 1991 when I was a managing director for the Investment Bank Salomon Brothers and running one of their European businesses, the company endured a near-death experience. A group of Salomon Brothers traders in New York had conducted illegal activities, to profit from a U.S. Treasury Bond auction. They had successfully made dozens of millions of dollars by the activity, but were eventually caught.

An indictment of the firm would have shut down the entire multi-billion dollar company. The market responded immediately and, because of the potential risk involved, funding for the company dried up. Quick action and support encouraged by the Treasury and the U.S. Federal Reserve saved the company. But, because of just a few in one location, a global, multi-business American financial standard bearer almost disappeared. Once again, the perception of weakness became reality.

Markets go up and down, and the business cycle continues. Dynamic, growing capitalism creates what the Austrian economist Joseph Schumpeter called "creative destruction." The markets become overly enthusiastic and over commit capital during optimistic cycles. Then they become overly negative and destroy good businesses during the down cycles. The good news is that this sort of volatility creates dynamism, with new winners and better opportunities in each cycle. As the old joke goes, the stock market has completely and accurately discounted six of the last three recessions—meaning that the market often mystifies the naysayers. Despite the prophets of doom on Wall Street and beyond, the economy in the first decade of the twenty-first century remains stronger than many people think, and with some perspective we can see that fact. Whatever the current emotional state of the financial wizards and the 24/7 financial news analysts, the economy remains strong, and America is still number one.

If Joseph Schumpeter was right and the cyclical nature of the markets creates positive momentum, we will see this positive long term impact eventually in the mortgage markets as well. The explosion of sub prime lending over the past several years has put many homeowners at risk as they stretched to buy homes that were expensive compared to their income. News of a larger than normal number mortgages going into default as these homeowners ran into financial difficulties led predictably to the *perception* of accelerating weakness. The "creative destruction" that hit the markets at that point led to the destruction of a lot of bank capital; but after all was said and done, many people who could never have bought a home without a sub prime boom ended up owning a home.

Even in the midst of the turmoil, it's a safe bet that America will continue to move toward a higher ratio of home ownership in the months and years ahead. We don't know that for a fact just yet, but we can see that the underlying economy is strong, and that's a good sign. And what we do know is that, whatever the current weakness, over time American resilience will prevail. During the last seven years the American economy has outperformed the majority of developed countries, and that momentum is a sure sign of strength.

2

Carrying the Tax Load

CONVENTIONAL WISDOM

Bush's tax cuts and military spending have created an astronomical U.S. budget deficit.

Typical Headlines

"Bush Deficit Cut Seen as Flawed"
—*New York Times, Sep. 8, 2004*

"Cost of Iraq War Could Surpass $1 Trillion"
—*MSNBC, Mar. 17, 2006*

"U.S. Government Debt Soars"
—*CNN, Dec. 3, 2007*

Facts

The average federal budget deficit over the past six years is 1.8% of GDP. This is below the average of the 70s (2.1%), 80s (3.0%), and 90s (2.2%). By the end of 2007 the deficit had dropped to 1.2%. Defense

U.S. Federal Deficit - % of GDF

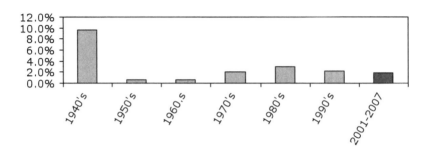

spending averaged 3.8% of GDP from 2002 to 2007, which is below the averages of the 40s, 50s, 60s, 70s, 80s, and 90s.

We're often reminded by the press of the enormous amounts being spent in Iraq and Afghanistan. The overall impression can be misleading, though, because separate votes each year in Congress mean the spending amounts are highlighted even though much of the spending would be incurred whether the wars were going on or not.

For perspective, there are 2.8 million men and women in the U.S. military today. The number of servicemen in Iraq is approximately 150,000 (that's 5% of the total of uniformed personnel.). If these soldiers were not in Iraq, they would be somewhere else. They would be clothed, fed, and using fuel and ammunition in training and preparedness exercises. The total costs involved would be less, but certainly not zero. Thus "war spending" sounds like it is all extra when it's really not.

Federal taxes, as a percent of total income, have *increased* during the Bush administration compared with the end of the Clinton administration. How is this possible? We have heard *endlessly* about Bush's tax cuts. While it's true that tax rates were reduced, when incomes increase, as they have, many households advance to higher tax brackets. Additionally, significant increases in U.S. corporate profits has led to increases in the taxes paid by corporations. (See, for example, information regarding taxes paid by ExxonMobil in Chapter 10).

The U.S.'s federal debt is $9 trillion. This is the largest debt of any nation by far and is a result of many years of budget deficits. It means that 10% of the U.S. budget goes to pay interest on the debt owed by the U.S. government to others.

However . . .

As a percent of GDP, the debt is lower today (65.5%) than in 1996 (67.3%). The debt to GDP ratio is relevant because the size of the economy is what determines the country's ability to pay the interest on its debt. In other words, the rise in profitability overall provides the capital businesses will use to pay off loans and continue producing goods and services. The U.S. debt is also lower than many developed countries and most developing countries as a percentage of annual income.

According to the IMF World Economic Outlook 2007, the US level of debt looks lower than the headlines indicate and the average of other developed economies. The IMF adjusts debt for a nation's liquid assets and shows the US debt level at just 44% of GDP. That compares to Japan at 90%, Italy at 100%, Germany at 57%, and France at 54%. Great Britain was at 38% and Canada, benefiting from the commodity

> ### Key Terms
>
> **Budget Deficit:** When the government takes in less money through taxes than it spends, this is a deficit. A budget surplus occurs when the government takes in more than it spends.
>
> **Federal Debt:** The cumulative effect of budget deficits or surpluses. After a deficit of $1 billion per year for five years, the federal debt would be $5 billion.
>
> **Trade Deficit:** When the people of a country buy more than they sell, this results in a trade deficit. Adam Smith argued that a trade deficit is not bad because when currency is exchanged for goals, by definition the trade is balanced. Each party got what it considered a fair deal.

boom, has dropped its debt to GDP down to ratio of 25%. (The IMF does not report comparable information for other countries.)

CONVENTIONAL WISDOM
Bush unfairly cut taxes only for the rich.

Typical Headlines

Bush Priorities Will Swell Deficit
—*Forbes, Jan. 10, 2006*

"Tax Cuts Offer Most for Very Rich, Study Says"
—*New York Times, Jan. 8, 2007*

"Democrats in Debate Urge Taxes on Rich"
—*AP, Dec. 14, 2007*

Facts
The fact is, just 1% of taxpayers pay 40% of federal income taxes in this country. This is an all time high and it is up from 34% in 2002, and 26% in 1986. An all time high 86% of income taxes are paid by the top 25% of income earners. This is up from 83% in 2001, and 76% in 1986. And it's equally impressive to note that an all time high 97% of income taxes are paid by the top 50% of earners. This is up from 94% in 2002 and 93.5% in 1986.

Obviously, taxes cannot be reduced without a disproportionate reduction for top earners. Since most taxes are paid by the wealthy, even a tax cut that would result in a more progressive schedule has a higher dollar savings for high-income taxpayers than for low-income taxpayers. A more progressive tax rate is one that proposes to cut tax rates for low-income taxpayers by more than the reduction for high-income taxpayers.

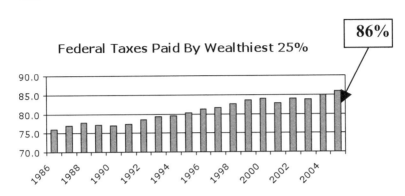

SOURCE: SOI BULLETIN, INDIVIDUAL INCOME TAX RATES AND TAX SHARES (1986–2005)[1]

President Bush's tax cuts reduced the top rate from 39% to 35%. The good news is that lots of people benefited from increasing growth and moved up into the top 35% bracket—so many, in fact, that tax revenues have gone up significantly, mostly from the highest earners. From 2000 to 2007, tax receipts from individuals increased by $164 billion. Corporate and other tax receipts went up another $350 billion. The tax amount paid by the top 25% of earners increased by $167 billion, while the remaining 75% of taxpayers paid $3 billion less in 2007 than in 2000.

Any way you slice it, these are not "huge tax cuts for the rich."

Assessment

The Principle is Simple:

1. With lower tax rates, more money goes into the economy. Money is spent; people are hired; money is invested; salaries go up. Things work.
2. With higher tax rates, more money goes to the government—a graveyard of bureaucracy and inefficiency.

The evidence has never been clearer. The U.S. economy grew by $3.8 trillion in six years. The federal government takes in about 20%

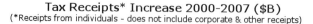

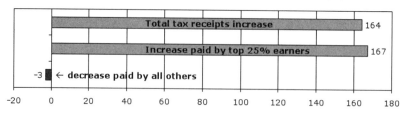

SOURCE: GAO: FEDERAL AND STATE AND LOCAL GOVERNMENT CURRENT RECEIPTS AND
EXPENDITURES, NATIONAL INCOME AND PRODUCT ACCOUNTS (NIPA), BY MAJOR TYPE
(1959–2007) [HTTP://WWW.GPOACCESS.GOV/EOP/TABLES08.HTML]. NOTE ALSO THAT
THE DATA SHOWN HERE REFLECT 2005 CENSUS DATA WITH 2007 TAX AMOUNTS.

of that increase, or $760 billion per year. If spending had been held constant, the deficit, which peaked at $412 billion, would never have appeared.

The amount of money being taken in by the U.S. government is insane. It is much more than what is needed to do what a federal government ought to be doing. There is, therefore, no good reason for today's large budget deficit. It can and should be fixed simply by curbing spending rather than economy-damaging tax increases. The line-item veto would be one important step to help achieve that objective by cutting pork-barrel spending from the federal budget, and reducing wasted time, energy, and money. In our view, more Americans should be pushing for these spending reforms.

The national debt is a disgrace, given America's prosperity. There is no way a country this rich should be in debt. The problem should be fixed. Nevertheless, it is not the cause for alarm that many would have us believe. The U.S.'s debt servicing cost of 10% of revenues is below the average U.S. household (12% to 14%) and about on par with the average business. As pointed out earlier in this chapter, the U.S. debt ratio looks very reasonable compared to the situation in Europe and, in fact, compared to most of the Organization for Economic Cooperation and Development (OECD) countries.

But this is an area where a little perspective may help. Defending this country is Job Number One. Given the fact that we're in the midst of a global war against fanatics whose stated mission is to destroy the U.S., western culture, democracy, and Christianity, spending 20% of the federal government's budget (about 3.8% of GDP) on national defense does not really seem all that high.

3

China in Perspective

CONVENTIONAL WISDOM

China's economic growth threatens the U.S. economy and its global economic lead.

Typical Headlines

"Stocks sink on fears about China and growth"
—*Reuters, Feb. 27, 2007*

"China growth extracting too high a toll"
—*Forbes, Oct. 14, 2007*

"China replaces U.S. as steadying force"
—*The Guardian, Oct. 18, 2007*

Facts

The growth of the U.S. economy since the beginning of the Bush administration is about equal to the entire economy of China. Go ahead, read that sentence again. Yes, it's true. Said another way, the

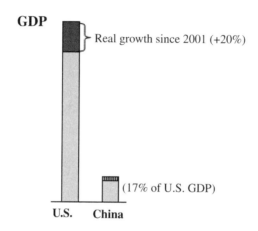

GDP

Real growth since 2001 (+20%)

(17% of U.S. GDP)

U.S.   China

amount of GDP added to the U.S. economy in just the past six years equals the entire Gross Domestic Product of China.

Keep in mind, the population of China is four times that of the U.S. So, if this chart were drawn on a per capita basis, the bar on the right would actually be one quarter of the height shown in this chart. The average American worker earns 22 times as much as the average Chinese worker.

Assessment

Is it not hard to believe that Americans feel economically threatened by a country where the average worker earns less than 5% of the average American? The idea that Americans are "unhappy with the economy" is beyond belief. Stop by Wal-Mart any day of the week and watch the shopping carts, loaded with products made in Asia. Americans who complain about the disappointing economy are buying such quantities of electronics, toys, sporting goods, clothing, and gadgets that they can hardly fit them into their ever expanding houses. They're able to buy all these goods because they just happened to be born on a piece of real estate called the United States where the advances made by three centuries of productive workers and free enterprise created a huge disparity between U.S. wages and that of China where the goods are made. So Asian workers get to make all these goods, and Americans get to buy them at a fraction of what they would cost if they had to make them themselves. Imagine what these goods would cost if they were made by U.S. companies paying 22 times the labor rate, not to mention the fact that with U.S. unemployment near 5%, even if we wanted to make these products in the U.S., there would be not be enough workers to do it!

The astonishing bounty available to the people of this nation should be a source of perpetual thanksgiving, not whining and dissatisfaction. Yet, according to a report from the Bloomberg financial news service, the growing size and affluence of Chinese manufacturing is seen by many, both in this country and abroad, as a major threat. The writer says that, "China's emergence as a world trade powerhouse, blamed in the U.S. and Western Europe for the loss of thousands of factory jobs, is having an even more severe impact on developing nations." As a result of these concerns, market watchers tell us, support for free trade is dwindling in developing countries around the world, as manufacturers, labor unions, and regional governments begin seeking trade protection against Chinese competition.[1]

Facts

There's no question that China's manufacturing sector is prospering. From the beginning of economic reforms in 1979 through 2006, China's GDP grew at an average annual rate of 9.7%, and topped 11.4% in 2007. That's an astonishing pace. The size of China's national economy increased eleven-fold, its per capita GDP grew eight-fold. In just under three decades, China's world ranking for total trade went from twenty-seventh to third overall. However, if the U.S. were only to grow by 2% and China kept growing by 7%, it would still take China thirty-eight years to catch up with America, and sixty-two years to catch up on a per capita basis.

Some have expressed concern that China may overtake the United States as the world's largest trade economy in a few years, and could become the world's largest economy within the next two decades. Comparing the U.S. with China on a Purchasing Power Parity (PPP) basis, this may be possible, but given that the population is four times that of the U.S., the per-capita income would still have a long way to go. The unspoken fear seems to be that China's rise may signal the beginning of America's economic decline.

However, as recently as 2004, Chinese economists were expressing their own concerns that things were moving too fast. The country's financial commissars began taking steps to rein in the rapid pace of growth, worried that the acceleration of new business was overheated and unsustainable. An editorial in *China Daily* noted that, "China's economy is still investment-driven. But the increase in fixed-asset investment, which greatly promoted economic development over the past few years, cannot maintain the 26.7% growth rate it achieved last year."

That publication's editors feared that the energy for continuing such a spectacular rate of growth had been exhausted, and they indicated that some industries and industrial regions of the country were "haunted by excessive investment." It's obvious that China has reaped huge benefits from their foray into the world of free trade, as well as from their wary advance toward democratic institutions. But those most responsible for creating and maintaining economic stability in China remain cautious, knowing that an overly aggressive posture—both internally and toward their global trading partners such as the United States—could be disastrous.

As the *Daily*'s editors observed, "Fast, stable and sustainable development is the basic characteristic of the new economic trend we are trying to sustain." To accomplish that goal, China's central bank issued new policies on mortgage loans and raised reserve requirements for commercial lending eight times in 2007 alone, a move aimed at absorbing liquidity in the banking system and curbing excessive credit growth. Analysts believe these moves, along with current bank reserve requirements of 17.5% (as of June 2008), will freeze more than $27 billion in the banking system slowing economic growth. Overseas China watchers hope these changes will restrain the "overheated growth" and provide long-term stability.[2]

Assessment

It should now be obvious that economic activity is not a zero-sum game. China's growth does not come at the expense of the U.S. growth. In fact, the reverse is more likely to be correct; when one country grows, it tends to spur growth in other countries, especially its trading partners. In 2007 and early 2008, export growth was a considerable boon to U.S. GDP growth. The progress of emerging countries is good for the U.S. because (a) their growth makes them larger markets in which the U.S. can sell goods and services, and (b) countries are far less likely to go to war with trading partners as the cost of conflict to the population is too high. Yes, their growth puts added demand on limited resources and pressure on the environment. These are issues that must be addressed with or without the growth of emerging countries.

Key Term

Purchasing Power Parity: A purchasing power parity (PPP) *exchange rate* equalizes the purchasing power of different *currencies* in their home countries for a given basket of goods. It is often used to compare the *standards of living* between countries, rather than a comparison at market exchange rates. It may reflect, for example, that even though a country's currency may be cheap in currency markets, the cost of locally purchased items like rice or haircuts allows them to live at a standard higher than market exchange indicates. It does not accurately reflect what would happen if a person were to sell his possessions and move to another country.

CONVENTIONAL WISDOM

China's industrial and economic growth is unstoppable, and America can't keep up

Typical Headlines

"China Emerges as Global Consumer"
—*BBC News, Feb. 17, 2005*

"U.N. Report Predicts U.S. Economy Will Lag"
—*Associated Press, Sept. 5, 2007*

"China Growth to Keep Commodity Boom Alive"
—*Reuters, May 13, 2008*

Facts

It's true that China's economic and industrial strength is growing at a very fast pace. However, there is strong evidence that the pace is unsustainable because it is growing without appropriate concern for public safety, for energy conservation, or for the environment, and this is becoming a source of concern both inside and outside China. Growth is good, but it must be at a rate the economy can naturally sustain.

In the mid-1990s, the U.S. and China both produced about 13% of the global steel supply. By mid-2007, the U.S. had dropped to 8% of global steel supply and China had increased its proportion to 35%. The massive internal construction drive in China has resulted in Chinese factories now producing 50% of all the flat glass and cement in the world. As the new Chinese middle class takes to the new roads, China has replaced Japan as the second largest manufacturer of new cars, while the U.S. holds on to its number one ranking. This growth has also increased China's demand to import foreign goods and commodities.

To support this rapid growth, however, China has had to produce more power. In 2005, China added as much electricity to its grid as Britain produces each year—66 gigawatts. In 2006, China increased output by 102 gigawatts, an amount equivalent to the annual energy production of France. In 2007, as evidence of continued growth in energy demand China burned 18% more coal than the prior year. Coal is the source of two-thirds of China's energy production.[3] China had been an exporter of coal, but is now an importer.

The Charging Dragon

Every 10 days China adds a new coal power plant sufficient to provide energy to a city the size of Dallas. China has to burn more coal to provide energy for its growing industry and growing middle class. The middle class is buying refrigerators, appliances, and TV sets as it gains wealth. All this increases China's demand for power. The amount of coal burned by China each year is now more than the aggregate used each year by Japan, Europe, and the United States combined. At the end of the first quarter of 2008, the numbers for China's economic growth were equally impressive. China's Real GDP was up 10.6% from the prior year, above the government's own target. Meanwhile, industrial production was up 17.8% and retail sales were up an amazing 21.5%. This was all supported in the first quarter by foreign direct investment in Chinese companies, which was up 61% from the previous year.

The government has targeted 9% real growth through the next decade as it strives to bring more citizens into the urban middle class. That is a rate of growth 6% higher than the 3% rate of growth many experts consider sustainable over the long term for the U.S. Having completed the huge Three Rivers dam project, China now has one of the biggest public works programs in history on the drawing boards: a $60 billion network of canals, rivers, and lakes to be built from the

Yangtze River in the wet southern half of the country to the Yellow River, Beijing and the parched North.

The government will also have to build homes for the millions of people it plans on moving from the countryside closer to the jobs in the cities. In this process, China has already built 7.5 billion square feet of commercial and residential space in each of the last few years. That is construction equal each year to all the existing malls in the U.S. And on top of this, China's government has a goal of producing urban housing for 300 million of its citizens over the next twenty years as it plans on increasing urban population by over 50%.

China's program of growth has a reason, as well as a high cost. The new $60 billion water project is a necessity. China has over 20% of the world's people and just 7% of the world's water supply. Poor land management and excessive use raises the risk that much of northern China could become a desert if counteractive conservation measures aren't taken now. More than one hundred of China's six hundred cities already face extreme water shortages; yet, the government's plans for increased growth are still in place. And water pollution is so severe in some places that cities will lack safe drinking water unless sanitation systems and treatment facilities are established immediately.[4]

Chinese sources have also reported that enormous areas in the Chinese Great Lakes, as well as an estimated 30% of China's rivers, have been found to be too polluted to use for either agricultural or industrial purposes. And according to the World Bank, Chinese producers use from four to ten times as much water as European companies for the same output, because water is priced so cheaply and water use is so poorly monitored that few make any effort to conserve it or treat water after use.

But water is not the only resource at risk from excessive use. Energy is heavily subsidized by the Chinese government to support heavy industrial growth. In 2006, gasoline sold in China at just over

$2.00 per gallon, when the wholesale price was already over $2.50 in the U.S. Electricity is equally heavily subsidized and distributed by regulated Chinese utilities at prices well below common international costs. The ISI Group, a private economic research group, estimated in May 2008 that if oil stays at $130 per barrel, China's oil subsidy if not cut would cost the government over $60 billion in 2008. That would be well over 1.5% of China's GDP. These cost pressures did force the government to reduce, but not eliminate, the oil subsidy in June 2008.

The High Cost of Growth

Because there is no price incentive, there is no strong emphasis on the importance of conservation. Chinese steel producers, for example, use 20% more energy than the international standard for energy consumption to produce a ton of steel, and they do it with few pollution controls. Furthermore, China's massive building and construction projects use little insulation, often ignoring even Chinese regulations. Chinese buildings have so little insulation that they require double the energy to heat and cool as the Western standard.

China's coal plants in most cases have been built with outdated 1960s technology. Modern high pressure, high temperature coal plants would produce 20% to 50% more power per ton of coal. However, making these facilities more efficient would require the purchase of Western technology and would be considerably more expensive to build. The government has not been willing to take that step. The regulated cost of coal is so low that the provincial governments that control the construction and use of these coal plants have no reason to pay for better or more efficient technology. Such a move would have to come from increased imports of U.S. and western European technology.

But there is an even higher price to pay for this apparent lack of concern. The cost of coal and inefficient technology is not just the cost of the government subsidy. According to a 2007 World Bank report done in conjunction with the Chinese Environmental Protection Agency (SEPA), each year China suffers from 350,000 to 400,000 additional deaths due to outdoor pollution. Indoor pollution is estimated to cause another 300,000 deaths. Again the technology to diminish these problems would likely have to be purchased from more developed economies.

Polluted water is estimated to cause 60,000 deaths each year, 99 percent of China's 560 million urban residents breathe air that would be deemed unsafe by European standards. In Beijing, the PM10 (Particulate Micrograms per Cubic Meter, a measure of pollutants in the air) averages over 140. In the city of Dotang, in one of the coal producing provinces, the level sometime exceeds 350. The U.S. standard is 50, and the European requirement is below 40.

In 2002, in the run up to the Kyoto Protocol, China promised to reduce sulfur emissions by 10% over the next decade; however, by 2005, Chinese sulfur emissions were actually up 27%.[5] The U.S. in 2004 generated half the sulfur emissions of China's 22.5 million tons. In 2005, China is estimated to have released 26 million tons of sulfur. Even where pollution control equipment has been installed, it's still questionable whether or not the technology is being used. Pollution control equipment on coal generators are expensive to maintain, and they use enormous amounts of electricity that the utility could sell on the grid. Consequently, there's little incentive to actually use the equipment.

Chinese officials argue that it's unfair to try to limit their access to commodities or curb their production of greenhouse gases since they are merely trying to catch up with developed nations.

China's leaders apparently believe they have a right to increase consumption and pollution. Limiting their nation's carbon footprint, they say, is an unfair standard, and point out that, on a per capita basis, the United States has ten times the carbon footprint of China. However, that's a false comparison. According to the U.S. Department of Energy, based on estimates of pollution in 2004, the U.S. carbon produced per capita is just five times China's per capita carbon footprint. More importantly, based on 2004 GDP, the U.S. carbon impact per unit of GDP was actually 20% below that of China at that time. This means that the U.S. produces at least 20% more GDP for every unit of carbon produced than China.[6]

From 2000 to 2004, U.S. Real GDP was up 7% while U.S. carbon emissions were up less than 2%. During the same period, however, China increased Real GDP by 43% while carbon emissions increased by more than 50%. That is unsustainable and unrealistic growth that can have a long-term negative impact not only on China, but on the rest of the world as well.[7] It reflects China's priorities because many technologies are available to mitigate pollution but little money is invested. Growth at any cost is easier when you can ignore the human cost and suppress complaints. China is maintaining rapid growth with unsustainable policies that can only lead to long-term environmental damage.

But these problems haven't gone totally unnoticed by the Chinese government's Central Committee. When President Hu Jintao addressed a forum of the ruling Communist Party in October 2007, he acknowledged what the world now knows, that China's economic growth is exacting too high a cost on energy resources, on the environment, and on Chinese society, and he indicated that the government will need to seek a more balanced economic model. Hu's remarks were reported by Chinese and Western media. But it remains to be seen whether or not the promise of more responsible growth will actually be carried out.

In spring 2008, when Chinese Premier Wen Jiabao spoke to the National People's Congress, his comments on the economy did not focus on the high cost of pollution. Rather, they were concerned about controlling inflation and continuing the government subsidies to industry.[8] The Chinese government considers the social unrest of the early 1990s to have been the result of inflation spiking into the teens after the 1994 devaluation of the Yuan. In his remarks, the Premier said that regulators should try to hold inflation to the 2007 level of 4.7%. The goal seems unlikely, however, given that inflation topped 8.3 % in the first quarter of 2008. And that was before the May 2008 earthquake that has put even greater pressure on food prices.

Chinese economic statistics show that the inflation in April 2008 was driven by the rise in food prices. Food prices were up 22%, including a 68% jump in pork prices, a 46% increase in the cost of cooking oil, and a 13.6% rise in the cost of vegetables. The average person in China spends 30% of his household budget on food, with the poorest spending 50% or more. In the U.S., by contrast, the average person spends less than 6% of his budget on food. In addition to government's efforts to limit inflation—primarily by continuing subsidies and maintaining price controls—they've also announced plans to control growth by limiting bank credit and raising bank reserve requirements to 17.5% of deposits.

Assessment

The increasing inflation and the other problems that China is now facing are typical economic indicators that growth has exceeded the nation's manageable rate. China's ability to increase industrial capacity and provide trained employees for industry is now less than the nation's current growth rate. Government's response of maintaining energy price controls and introducing price controls on food are only likely to work in the short run if growth, in fact, drops to a sustainable rate.

The current rate of growth is also unsustainable based on the negative impact that the unregulated expansion is having on the environment. In a democratic country the painful cost of pollution would surely result in a public outcry and a change of government. China is a Communist government with absolute control of the press and a willing police state to suppress protest. Although technically communist, the regime is actually now a one party socialist state with significant portions of the economy controlled by independent enterprises. When the SEPA developed a "Green GDP" to account for the cost of pollution, the government didn't like the result and stopped any further publication of the calculation. The government moves hundreds of thousands of people to make way for dams and power projects but does not account for the negative impact of these projects on the environment or the displaced peoples' lives.

China will have to become enormously more productive, and not merely a bigger manufacturer to compete with the U.S. and maintain high levels of growth over a long period of time. Much of the technology and equipment to achieve this will have to be purchased from the developed world. Based on 2004 GDP numbers, China produced only 4% of the GDP per person that the U.S. produces.

To equal our own quality of life standards, the environment in China must first be saved. Its water must be drinkable and the air must be breathable. The government can suppress the complaints of its citizens, but it cannot deny the reality and economic impact forever. If China expects to rival the U.S. for quality of life and efficiency, it will need to radically shift its domestic policies and pricing structures. To improve real efficiency dramatically compared to the standard benchmarks of the OECD countries it envies, it will have to buy more western technology.

The world benefits from China's growth. More goods are available for consumers throughout the world at cheaper prices because of China's participation in world trade. But the rate of growth and sustainability of growth has real limits in China as in any country. China, if it acts wisely, will slow growth to a rate that allows it to manage the environmental impact and develop commodity resources as quickly as it builds commodity demand. China may have to focus more on quality of life rather than quantity of GDP to get to the next level of global competitiveness. In the short term China may have to look more to the U.S., or other developed countries to find the technology and systems it needs. Despite America's problems it is still a great example of balanced growth and industrial efficiency for China to copy.

4

Trade in Transition

CONVENTIONAL WISDOM

The U.S. has almost completely lost its manufacturing base to foreign countries. We've become just a "service economy."

Typical Headlines

"Loss of Manufacturing Base May Mean Loss of U.S. Power"
—*Milwaukee Journal-Sentinel, Jan. 6, 2003*

"China Overtakes U.S. as Tech Supplier"
—*International Herald-Tribune, Dec. 12, 2005*

"U.S. Manufacturing Keeps Losing Ground"
—*Pittsburgh Post-Gazette, Feb. 20, 2007*

Facts

Contrary to the common view, the U.S. is still the largest producer of industrial goods in the world. The U.S.'s $2.73 trillion in industrial output is double that of number two Japan's $1.36 trillion. The U.S.

has a manufacturing output of $1.73 trillion, compared to Japan's $953 billion and China's $760 billion. If agriculture, services, and government are included, total U.S. production is $12.4 trillion, and no other nation comes close.[1] The U.S. exports to many countries, most notably Canada and Mexico, both of which are partners in the North American Free Trade Agreement (NAFTA).

The U.S. trades with the entire world, and exports an enormous amount of manufactured goods—more than any other nation in the world. Although we often hear claims that the U.S. is rapidly becoming a service-based economy with minimal manufacturing and industrial output, that's simply not the case. Of the $1.62 trillion that the U.S. exported in 2007, nearly 70% of the total—or approximately $1.1 trillion—came from manufactured goods. Forgive the confusing category descriptions in the following chart, they are the result of 50 years of Commerce Department bureaucracy.

In most of the manufacturing categories representing the bulk of the U.S.'s output, the United States is at or near the top of the world in production. The table below lists manufactured goods produced in the United States, and the production value for the top 15 categories. The U.S. exports more today than at any other time in American history. Whether to our NAFTA partners, the EU, Japan, or the rest of the world, the United States is also exporting at record levels. Below is a table detailing growth of exports from 1962 to 2005. The chart shows just how much American exports to each of our trading partners has increased over the 43-year period, from 1962 to 2005.

Assessment

Yes, the number of manufacturing jobs has declined. But the value of U.S. manufactured goods has increased—significantly. We've produced more goods with fewer laborers (thus increasing productivity), and the resulting money has gone into the economy to hire people in

15 CATEGORIES ACCOUNT FOR NEARLY TWO-FIFTHS OF ALL U.S. MANUFACTURED GOODS EXPORTS

Electronic Integrated Circuits & Microassembly, and Parts	$46.30
Aircraft, Powered; Spacecraft and Launch Vehicles	$45.60
Motor Cars and Vehicles for Transporting Persons	$34.80
Parts & Accessories for Motor Vehicles (Head 8701-8705)	$33.70
Automatic Data Processing Machines; Magnetic Readers, etc.	$26.60
Turbojets, Turbopropellers and Other Gas Turbines, and Parts	$22.70
Parts, etc., for Typewriters and Other Office Machines	$21.00
Parts of Balloons, etc., Aircraft, Spacecraft, etc.	$20.70
Medical, Surgical, Dental, or Veterinary Instruments	$15.90
Medicaments Nesoi, Mixed or Not, in Dosage, etc.	$15.80
Parts for Machinery of Headings 8425 to 8430	$12.40
Motor Vehicles for Transport of Goods	$11.60
Electric Apparatus for Line Telephony, etc. and Parts	$11.00
Machines, etc., Having Individual Functions Nesoi, and Parts	$9.20
Transmission Apparatus for Radiotele., etc., TV Cameras	$8.40
SUBTOTAL:	**$335.90**

other jobs which are more interesting and create even more value. We know this is true since unemployment has been near historic lows. And you might find a few people who would rather be working on an assembly line all day than what they currently do, but that would be an isolated exception, not the rule. The aggregate view is most important as we consider the overall direction of the country. This positive scenario is VERY different from the one often portrayed by gloom and doomers who want to paint the economy as a failure by pointing to losses in manufacturing jobs. The cycle explained here is closely related to the concept explained in the next Chapter about why outsourcing is good for America.

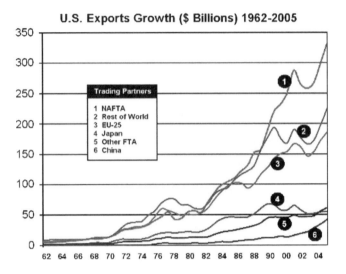

U.S. Exports Growth ($ Billions) 1962-2005

Trading Partners

1 NAFTA
2 Rest of World
3 EU-25
4 Japan
5 Other FTA
6 China

Key Terms

Manufacturing Output: Manufacturing output is the money value of goods produced in factories

Industrial Output: Industrial output is the money value of goods produced in factories plus mining, including oil and gas.

Balance of Trade: The balance of trade is the difference between the money value of exports and the money value of imports in the economy over a specific period of time. Trade deficit is a negative balance which results from a country importing more goods and services than it exports. Trade surplus is the reverse. The surplus is the result of a country exporting more goods and services than it imports.

Balance of Payments: The balance of payments is the overall sum of the flow of payments from an individual country with the rest of the world. In simpler terms, if an individual buys more goods and services than he can sell and accumulates a trade deficit, he will have to balance the deficit with a capital inflow. In balance of payments, the capital inflow is known as the "current account" or "capital account surplus"—which would be the equivalent of covering your deficit by borrowing from the bank or running up your credit card balance. The only other alternative is to spend money from your savings. For national accounts, the equivalent of running down savings is drawing on official central bank reserves.

Capital Account: The capital account is one of the two major components of the "balance of payments." It includes all transactions between a country and other countries. It deals with both direct investment, such as the purchasing of real estate or goods, or the changes in investment in stocks, bonds, and the like. A foreign investor buying assets domestically is considered a capital inflow, and the opposite is a capital outflow.

Current Account (Financial Account): A nation's current account is the difference between a nation's total exports of goods, services, and transfers, and its imports of the same things. Current account balances depend on the net foreign assets of a country, positive or negative, determining the balance.

CONVENTIONAL WISDOM

The U.S. trade deficit is out of control, and will soon create a huge financial disaster.

Typical Headlines

"Trade Deficit Leaps Again"
—*Washington Post, Jan. 13, 2005*

"Flirting With Deficit Disasters"
—*Washington Post, Mar. 16, 2005*

"U.S. Trade Gap Reaches All-Time High"
—*MSNBC, Apr. 12, 2005*

Facts

The U.S trade deficit has been around 5 to 6% of GDP for a number of years. This is high. In fact trade deficits of this level have caused economic crises in developing countries—such as Brazil in 1998 and 2002, and in Argentina in 2002. The fact that developing countries have been driven into economic crisis by large trade deficits is one of the main reasons the U.S. trade deficit generates concern, and why it's viewed as an unsustainable imbalance by many economists.

Over 40% of the U.S. deficit is due to oil imports. If oil is removed from the equation, the deficit is trending downward significantly. The non-oil deficit peaked in 2006 at 3.9% and is down to about 2.3%. Energy imports, America's dependence on foreign oil, is the main reason the trade deficit remains high.

Assessment

While recent trade deficits are a concern, the recent decline in the non-oil deficit shows the competitiveness of U.S. manufacturing. The

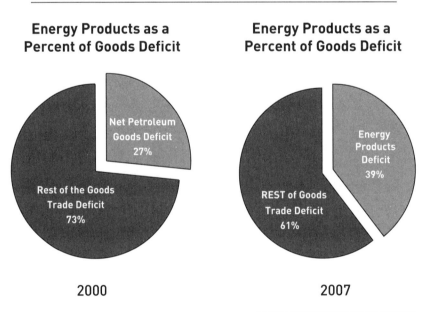

Energy Products as a Percent of Goods Deficit

Net Petroleum Goods Deficit 27%

Rest of the Goods Trade Deficit 73%

2000

Energy Products as a Percent of Goods Deficit

Energy Products Deficit 39%

REST of Goods Trade Deficit 61%

2007

SOURCE: BUREAU OF ECONOMIC ANALYSIS

deficit was being kept high by a dollar that was too strong, making U.S. exports too costly. Now that the dollar is at a more fair level, it is reasonable to expect that the non-oil deficit will return to the quite sustainable levels of about 1½% of GDP that existed in the early 1990's, but with normal economic lags that could take several years. The oil deficit will not be fixed by the currency adjustment.

Why did the recent deficit of +6%, which has spelled disaster for other countries, not do so for the U.S.? (see Chapter 7 for details.) It is partly because when the U.S. borrows and pays back debt, it is denominated in dollars—America's own currency. A developing country that borrows dollars to fund a deficit, but then pays back from an economy that operates in a currency that is rapidly depreciating against the dollar, is hit hard. This would be like borrowing money to buy an apartment building that has a stream of rental income and then having your income go down every year making it harder to pay back the loan. America does not face this problem; we borrow in dollars so the debt is stable in comparison to the income stream of our GDP.

More importantly, though, developing countries that run deficits often simultaneously invest unwisely. Fortunately, the U.S. has continued to invest in things that keep the productivity and competitiveness of the U.S. strong. This is why we are now seeing the non-oil deficit go down.

Facts

The table below shows that five of the countries with which the U.S. runs the largest deficits are all major oil exporters. The impact of oil makes it difficult to analyze the impact of regional trading on U.S. manufacturing trade under the NAFTA accords. (see Chapter 17)

Adding just three more trading partners accounts for more than 93% of the total U.S. trade deficit.

COUNTRY	% OF TRADE DEFICIT TO OCT 2007
Mexico	10.0%
Canada	9.4%
Nigeria	3.9%
Venezuela	3.8%
Saudi Arabia	3.4%
TOTAL	**30.5%**

The Impact of Overseas Dollar Reserves

COUNTRY	% OF TRADE DEFICIT TO OCT 2007
China	36.3 %
Japan	11.75%
Euro Zone	15.2%

Another key issue is that, over the past five years, the major oil-exporting nations and developing Asian countries have been active in preventing their currencies from appreciating against the dollar. Currency intervention by their central banks has effectively delayed a natural correction in the trade imbalance by preventing the cost of U.S. manufactured goods from becoming cheaper when compared to other nations' exports.

Asian export-based economies have acted aggressively to keep the dollar strong in order to hold down the cost of their own goods on the U.S. market. China alone has bought almost $1.6 trillion of capital reserves in U.S. dollars to slow the appreciation of the Yuan against the dollar, in an effort to maximize domestic Chinese industrial growth. In the early 2000s, Japan bought approximately $1 trillion in U.S. currency, which they still hold in reserves. By keeping their own currency weak and the dollar strong, Japan's Ministry of Finance hopes to prevent the extended recession and shrinking population from turning into a depression.

China is the lead actor in the move by Asian exporters to keep their currencies weak against the dollar and maximize their exports to the U.S. and other dollar-based economies. It's easier to see the impact of the Asian economies on the U.S. goods trade deficit if we examine the goods trade deficit excluding the portion of the goods deficit related to energy products (and oil in particular). The charts below show the non oil goods trade deficit that is explicitly related to China. If you added the other Asian exporters to the picture, it would be even more dramatically apparent that they create the manufacturing deficit.

2000 GOODS TRADEDEFICIT EXCLUDING ENERGY   **2007 GOODS TRADE DEFICIT EXCLUDING ENERGY**

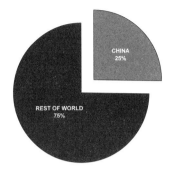

SOURCE: BUREAU OF ECONOMIC ANALYSIS

Assessment

The natural solution to a trade deficit is a weakening currency. When the U.S. maintains a trade deficit, this means that American companies are able to buy more foreign goods and services than foreign companies are willing to buy U.S. goods and services. In this situation, the U.S. consumer ends up with more things to consume, and the foreign companies end up holding extra dollars. In time, we would expect those foreign companies to sell their extra dollars to buy some of their own domestic currency and expand business in their home country. If they don't sell those dollars, they must invest them in the U.S., creating cheap capital to expand business in this country.

In fact, a significant reduction in the trade deficit of the U.S. with Canada and the Euro Zone countries has been achieved over the last few years. These are countries that don't manage their currencies. However, our trade deficits with the oil-producing countries and countries that have intervened in currency markets—including South Korea and especially China—have expanded. The trade deficit with Europe was $64 billion in 2001, and reached $122 billion in 2005, before falling back to $105 billion in 2007.

The U.S. will remain a manufacturing powerhouse. America can manage, and will benefit from further currency adjustments and further expansion of free trade. The free trade framework embodied in the World Trade Organization framework has kept inflation low and growth strong across the globe. The imbalances in the system are not the result of U.S. policy. The actions of countries to delay natural adjustments will eventually fail, and trade balances will adjust. In the end America will continue to enjoy cheap goods prices and strong growth of the global economy.

5

Outsourcing Is Good for America

CONVENTIONAL WISDOM

Good U.S. jobs are being outsourced to other countries, putting America's economic future at risk.

Typical Headlines

"Reverse Brain Drain Threatens U.S. Economy"
—*USA Today, Feb. 23, 2004*

"Labor, Jobs Headed Overseas"
—*New York Times, Aug. 8, 2004*

"China Outpaces U.S. in Exports"
—*Seattle Times, April 13, 2007*

In 2004, opponents of the move toward offshore alliances were saying that one of every ten jobs in the U.S. computer, software, and information technology industries would be going overseas in the near future. One in four IT jobs was predicted to go offshore by 2010. A report from Forrester Research concluded that, "at least 3.3 million white-collar jobs and $136 billion in wages will shift from the U.S. to low-cost countries like India, China, and Russia" by 2015.[1] Other analysts predicted that a large number of the 57 million white-collar and professional jobs in this country would suddenly be lost to overseas suppliers if the outsourcing trend continued.

Evidence of what could happen, they said, could be seen in the examples of Japan, Germany, and the United Kingdom, which were bleeding white-collar and technical jobs to lower-cost Asian nations. The UK alone was expected to send as many as 25,000 high-tech jobs, and 30,000 banking and finance jobs to India and other developing countries over the next five to ten years. By some estimates, Europe will lose more than a million such jobs to India and China by the year 2015.

Aware that job losses were real, as were concerns about the trade deficit, public discourse about outsourcing and trade became major campaign issues. *Business Week* reported in 2004 that not everyone was happy with the numbers coming from Washington. "The link between strong growth and job creation appears to be broken," the writer observed, "and we don't know what's wrong with it. Profits are soaring, yet no one is hiring. Angry voices are blaming Benedict Arnold CEOs who send jobs to India and China. If highly educated 'knowledge' workers in Silicon Valley are losing their jobs," he added, "who is really safe?"[2]

It sounded like a rebellion in the making. This fear came at the height of the political season, despite the fact that the GDP was above what the Federal Reserve Bank thinks is a sustainable rate of growth, advancing at a rate of 3.4%. The unemployment rate was dropping and was already down to 5.5% from a high of over 6% during the recession. The transition from 2004 to today tells much the same story. Politicians campaigning in Ohio, Michigan, and Illinois have blamed job losses on outsourcing and bad trade deals. Outsourcing is feared, and heartrending stories about families devastated by lost jobs remain common in the press. Those who have lost jobs in Michigan or Indiana won't necessarily appreciate the job gains in Louisiana and Arkansas, but markets and marketplace conditions change, and that's simply a fact of doing business in the twenty-first century. And while these changes will bring about a redistribution of the labor force, the job market in this country is still strong and growing.

Facts

The simple fact is that from 2000 to the end of 2007 there were 8.3 million new jobs created and unemployment was very low, while many jobs (good estimates are not readily available) were outsourced to India and other countries. The 5.2% average unemployment rate should be sufficient evidence to demonstrate that outsourcing is not necessarily bad for the U.S. To understand this seeming paradox, consider the following extreme but analogous situation where the U.S. lost 82% of its jobs . . . and it turned out to be a good thing. In 1820, 85% of the U.S. jobs were in farming. As a result of efficiency improvements, today that number is just 3%,[3] meaning that approximately 82% of American jobs went away. Why was this good? Because the U.S. now gets all the food it needs from just 3% of its workers, *plus* it gets all the additional things created by the 82% who would have been farming, but who are now making automobiles, golf clubs, fitness machines, household products, medicines, and countless other goods and services that make our lives better.

While this is undeniably good in the long run, it must be acknowledged that some people experienced hardships during the shrinkage from 85% to 3%. Those hardships however, were generally short term, as the individuals made the transition from one sector of the economy to another, and those hardships must be weighed against the greater good. Between 1860 and 1920, the number of factory workers went from 1.3 million to nearly 10 million, and output grew from $854 million to $24 billion. By the 1890s the manufacturing sector in this country had surpassed agriculture as the primary source of income for American workers. And by 1920, man-ufacturing productivity was more than twice that of the farm-based economy.

Assessment

Outsourcing seems bad only if we think of jobs in a narrow sense as work in exchange for money. This leads to a simplistic notion that there is a limited amount of money to go around, so work done by a foreigner must be at the expense of work done by an American. But to understand the big picture, we must think of work as being part of the process of creating something of value, some of which goes to the worker when the product or service is sold. If the work can be done for less by some-one in another country, freeing up American time to do other things of greater value, the total amount of value to be enjoyed by Americans is increased.

Facts

Both Non-Farm Payroll records and the Bureau of Labor Statistics Household Survey report total job growth from 2000 to the end of 2007 of .8% to 1.2 % per annum, close to the growth rate of the working age population. Employment has been fairly stable, with consistently low levels of unemployment. While U.S. real GDP growth did indeed slow to 0.6% in the fourth quarter of 2007 and the first quarter of 2008—down from 4.9% in the third quarter of 2007—the underlying industrial economy was nevertheless hum-ming along at a steady pace. Outside the housing industry, the bal-ance of the U.S. economy was continuing as it had done throughout the past six years. While employers in some sectors had been slower to add employees than in previous recoveries, they're also reluctant to let them go.

As the fear of outsourcing peaked in 2004, *Business Week*'s ana-lysts responded more thoughtfully to the issue that while jobs were growing, they were not growing as fast as in previous growth cycles, saying that, "The real culprit in this jobless recovery is productivity, not off-shoring. Unlike most previous business cycles, productivity has continued to grow at a fast pace right through the downturn and into recovery." The article points out, further, that just one percentage point in productivity growth could eliminate as many as 1.3 million jobs in a single year. Based on this assumption, the actual productivity gains of 2.6% per year during the Bush Administration might have destroyed 24 million jobs. But that didn't happen. Higher productivity didn't lead to fewer jobs, rather it enabled more output of goods for the American consumer.[4] The higher productivity allowed for increases in US output exceeding population growth and therefore increased incomes and wealth. Unemployment continued to fall to historic lows. In fact, from 2000 through 2008, despite a recession, terrorist attacks in New York and Washington, and back-to-back hurricanes, the U.S. added more than 5 million new jobs.

Even as the economy's growth slowed in the second quarter of 2008, the Federal Reserve's "Beige Book" still reported that employers had shortages of skilled workers in industries outside finance and real estate, the two areas most hurt by the collapse of sub prime mortgages.[5]

Assessment

The history of business is littered with the remains of those who couldn't change with the times—buggy-whip makers, steamship builders, coal-burning locomotive manufacturers, and photographic film producers are no longer in high demand. Trade and outsourcing in the twenty-first century may appear different than the kinds of changes seen before, but they are in effect the same. Changes like this can be unsettling, but they inevitably demonstrate America's strength and its ability to excel when challenged. Americas resilient and flexible system has consistently enabled it to surpass other developed countries through repeated cycles of change.

Key Terms

Insourcing: Insourcing is when a non-U.S. company moves facilities that provide goods and services from outside the U.S. into the borders of the U.S.

Outsourcing: Outsourcing occurs when a company closes a department or part of a department, and then contracts to have that unit's product or service provided by a group outside the company, and separate from the company. This is usually done to lower costs of production by moving the production elsewhere, or to create better efficiencies by allowing management to focus its energy on its core skill set. The term outsourcing is often used to mean moving jobs offshore, even though it can also mean moving jobs to an external company within the U.S.

Offshoring: Offshoring is outsourcing when the domestic department or part of a department is closed to move the production of goods or services outside the borders of the United States. The purpose of doing this is usually the same as outsourcing, but often the new offshore entity providing the service may still be owned by the U.S. company.

6

Understanding Inequality

CONVENTIONAL WISDOM

The middle class has not benefited from the recent growth in the economy.

Typical Headlines

"Connecting the Dots from Tax Cuts for the Rich to Loss of Benefits"
—*New York Times, Oct. 16, 2003*

"Current Government 'robbing the hood'"
—*USA Today, Jul, 27, 2006*

"Obama Addresses Income Inequality"
—*Washington Post, Nov. 8, 2007*

Facts

1. Real after-tax per capita personal income rose by 12.1%—an average of more than $3,700 per person during the past seven years.[1]
2. Real wages (pre-tax) have risen by 3.6 percent.[2]
3. Non-salaried wages increased more than salaried earnings (+24% vs. +22.1%) over the past seven years.[3]
4. The unemployment rate has been around 5% below the averages for the past three decades.
5. The U.S. economy added more than 8.3 million jobs from August 2003 through the end of 2007.

The most important way that middle income Americans benefit from economic strength is by jobs being available if they want them. Low unemployment trumps income growth. Clearly, with nearly record low unemployment, this requirement has been met.

What do we know about "middle-class income?" This simple question seems like it should be easy to answer, but it is the subject of many widely-reported fallacies. When you see claims that household income has been stagnant, this is because the average household size has been declining. The fact is that the average real household income rose by only 6% from 1969 to 1996, and to most that sounds like stagnation. But in the same amount of time real income per *person* rose by 51%.[4]

When you see claims that the American middle class is vanishing, to a degree this is true but it is statement designed for its political spin not to enlighten people. The middle class is shrinking because many in the range that would have been considered middle class have moved up to a higher income level, leaving fewer in the lower income range.

Further, true wage advances tend to be understated because they do not include the value of health insurance and retirement benefits which have been increasing rapidly, and because the number of part-timers has been increasing and their wages are lumped in with the totals.[5] For an excellent review of these and other fallacies about middle class income and income stagnation, see Thomas Sowell's *Economic Facts and Fallacies*.

The truth is, most people are making more money today, and they're better off than ever before. Real median household income in the United States reached an all-time high of $48,200 in 2006, median household family income, while averages in multi income families are up to $60,000 and for most Americans the trend continues upward. While definitions of poverty rate tend to be somewhat specious, the nation's official poverty rate declined for the first time this decade, from 12.6% in 2005 to 12.3% in 2006.[6]

Assessment

Next time you hear someone say its harder for the average family to make ends meet than it was thirty years ago, ask them how they're doing with their flat panel TV, ninety-six cable channels, personal computer and high speed internet, iPod, and air conditioning, all of which are good examples of the many, many things that have been added to the inventory of a typical household over and above what was there thirty years ago. The claim is emotive and cries out to the ever increasing wealth of the American Dream, but it does not reflect economic reality.

CONVENTIONAL WISDOM

Tax cuts for the rich have pushed income inequality up rapidly to record levels.

Typical Headlines

"Americans Fear New Tax Cuts Will Unfairly Benefit the Rich"
    —*Wall Street Journal, Jun. 20, 2003*

"Big Gain for Rich Seen in Tax Cuts for Investments"
    —*New York Times, Apr. 5, 2006*

"Tax Cuts Offer Most for Very Rich, Study Says"
    —*New York Times, Jan. 8, 2007*

Facts

The most common measure of income inequality is the Gini Index, a calculation that captures in one number the difference between actual income distribution and perfectly even income distribution. The Gini Index summarizes the dispersion of income and ranges from 0, or perfect equality, to 1, or perfect inequality.

Perfect equality corresponds to a GINI index of 0. In this scenario the top 1% of population receive 1% of income and the bottom 1% of the population also get 1% of income. A GINI index near 1 would be extreme inequality, for example the top 1% of the population receives 99% of the income and the remaining 99% of the people have to share out the remaining 1% of the income.

After increasing for 25 years, income inequality in the U.S. was essentially stable from 2001—2005, the latest year for which information is available. The Gini Index increased from 0.386 to 0.466 between 1969 and 2001. Since then it has averaged 0.466, with the latest figure at 0.470 (+0.004 over four years). What this tells us that the increase in income disparity in four years was so small it is not visible on a chart showing the Gini index for the two years. (See the charts in the appendix.)

The questions remain though, what caused the long-term increase in income inequality, and is it reason for concern? Former Federal Reserve Chairman Alan Greenspan writes in his book, *The Age of Turbulence: Adventures in a New World*, that the increase in income disparity from 1980 to 2003 is troublesome. This comment was widely reported in the press, but his explanation for the increase and the reason for his concern were not.

Greenspan's explanation is very different from the conventional wisdom that tax cuts for the rich caused the increase in disparity. (It should be evident from our analysis in Chapter 2 that this could not mathematically be the case.) Rather, he points to differences in educational standards between rich and poor as the culprit, and his recommended solution is to improve the quality of education for all Americans in order to provide advancement through educational opportunities for the poor. The reason for Greenspan's concern about increasing disparity is that lower income earners would pressure legislators to implement misguided policies purely out of their resentment for the rich.

The International Monetary Fund points to a different but related cause for increasing disparity. According to a lengthy study by the IMF, "per capita incomes have also risen across virtually all regions for even the poorest segments of the world's population, indicating that the poor are better off in an absolute sense . . . although incomes for the relatively well off have increased at a faster pace."[8] They observed that income disparity has been on the rise everywhere, not just in the U.S., and they trace the increase to differences in the availability of technology. Quite simply, the more education and technical skill a person possesses, the better off financially he or she is likely to be.

Assessment

Blaming increases in income disparity on recent tax policies is false and leads to misguided solutions. The solution is to address the causes and improve education and technology availability among the poor.

CONVENTIONAL WISDOM

It's true what we've always heard: poor people are doomed to stay poor while the rich get richer.

Typical Headlines

"Report Says That the Rich Are Getting Richer Faster, Much Faster"
—*New York Times, Dec. 15, 2007*

"Yawning Rich-Poor Gap Could Hobble Economy"
—*Christian Science Monitor, July 30, 2007*

Facts

Income and social-class mobility are alive and well in the United States, as indicated by several recent studies. A 2007 Report from the Department of the Treasury, based on the examination of federal income tax returns from 1987 and 1996, reported that more than half of U.S. households (56% by one measure and 57% by another) moved to a higher or lower income quintile between 1987 and 1996. Approximately half of households initially in the bottom 20% of the population moved to a higher quintile within ten years. The largest percentage increases in real incomes were, in fact, earned by those who started out in the lowest income groups.[9]

A separate study by the U.S. Census Bureau published in 1998 reported that, on average, more than 41% of Americans increased their inflation-adjusted income by 5% or more per year from 1984 to 1994. The primary reasons for the change in income from year to year was either a change in marital status, a change in the number of workers in the household, or moving into or out of full-time, year-round employment.[10] A study by the Economic Policy Institute in 2000 showed that almost 60% of Americans in the lowest income quintile in 1969 were in a higher quintile in 1996, while over 61% in the highest income quintile had moved down into a lower income quintile during the same period.[11]

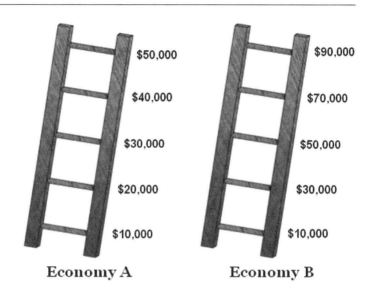

Economy A	Economy B
$50,000	$90,000
$40,000	$70,000
$30,000	$50,000
$20,000	$30,000
$10,000	$10,000

Assessment

Is there a substantial difference in income between rich and poor in this and all countries? Yes, but that's the wrong question. The correct question is: "Can the poor improve their lot? And, are they doing it now?" That is, can the poor move up the income ladder?

Here's one way to look at it. Imagine that you have a choice between being in the bottom income quintile in two different countries. In Economy A (as shown in the diagram) the bottom quintile earns an average of $10,000 a year and the middle quintile earns $30,000. In Economy B, the bottom and middle quintiles earn averages of $10,000 and $50,000 respectively. So which one would you choose?

If you can move up the quintile ladder, certainly Economy B is the better choice. If you can't move up, Economy B is still better because when the higher quintiles spend money, it fuels the economy and the rung you're on is likely to go up more than it will in Economy A. The only reason you might prefer Economy A is if envy is more important to you than opportunity.

The U.S. is the land of opportunity and everyone has a chance to move up, so long as they demonstrate the capacity to learn and improve. Most people begin on the first rung. They are likely to move up over time. And in time some individuals or their children will make it to the level of Donald Trump or possibly even Bill Gates, and that's a good thing. Individuals at that level of income spend a lot of money to build the economy, and people like Bill Gates give away a lot of their money to help other people achieve wonderful things. Why would anyone want that to change?

7

The Dynamic Dollar

CONVENTIONAL WISDOM

The declining value of the dollar is the result of government misman-agement. It's more evidence of America's decline.

Typical Headlines

"Dollar Expected to Fall Further"
    —*USA Today, Nov. 24, 2004*

"The American Empire is Falling With the Dollar"
    —*Online Journal, Nov. 8, 2007*

"Dollar Collapse Crippling U.S. Power"
    —*Newsweek, Nov. 23, 2007*

Facts

The dollar is, in fact, weak against the Euro and some major curren-cies. This is helping the U.S. increase exports, which added 1% to the U.S. GDP in 2007 over 2006. However, the dollar is still strong

against the Asian countries which export significant amounts of goods
to the U.S. and other countries.

To keep the dollar expensive and their own currencies weak, these
exporting countries have bought over 4 trillion U.S. dollars in recent
years. This purchase of dollars keeps their products cheap, and thus
their exports strong. But such large dollar purchases represent huge
sums for these countries, both on an absolute basis and relative to the
size of their economies. The resulting enormous dollar holdings represent a significant risk for them; if the dollar continues to decline to
what the IMF considers to be a fair value against their currencies, the
cost to them would be high. The Chart below shows the yearly rise or
fall of the Dollar against the European common currency the Euro.

The dollar is so expensive against the Asian currencies by the IMF
Purchasing Power Parity (PPP) measure that, despite the dollar being
weak against Europe, the dollar still remains strong against the world,
on average. The IMF 2008 "World Economic Outlook," published in
April 2008 says, "The analysis of the Consultative Group on Exchange

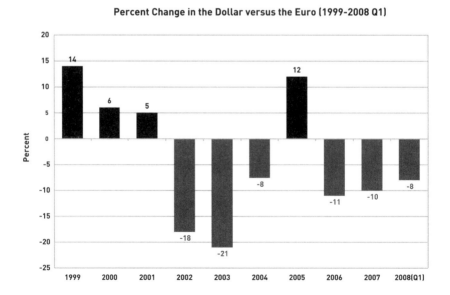

Percent Change in the Dollar versus the Euro (1999-2008 Q1)

MAJOR OVERSEAS DOLLAR RESERVE

COUNTRY		GDP (BILLIONS)	FOREIGN EXCHANGE RESERVES
Hong Kong	73%	207	152
Taiwan	81%	353	289
Russia	38%	1,289	493
China	52%	3,250	1,682
India	28%	1,098	303
South Korea	27%	957	260
Japan	22%	4,383	977
Brazil	15%	1,313	198

GDP from IMF 2008 World Economic Outlook

Foreign Exchange reserves from Bloomberg news APRIL 30, 2008

Rate Issues (CGER) of the IMF suggests that the U.S. dollar has now moved closer to its medium-term equilibrium level but still remains somewhat on the strong side."

An adjustment in the dollar exchange rate implied by the IMF Purchasing Power Parity would strongly increase U.S. GDP growth as the trade balance improved but could cause inflationary issues. In the following table a positive number represents how much a currency would have to appreciate against the dollar to reach purchasing power parity versus the dollar. A negative number represents how much another country's currency would have to drop to reach purchasing power parity against the dollar to be fairly priced.

The Dollar's Weakness Against Europe

The dollar has weakened dramatically since 2001. This is mostly the result of an overvaluation in 2001 when the dollar was expensive on every measure against most currencies. An in depth analysis of the IMF Purchasing Power Parity demonstrated the dollar's overvaluation

DOLLAR OVER VALUATIONS

COUNTRY	CURRENT DOLLAR GDP	PPP GDP	IMPLIED DOLLAR OVER VALUATION
India	1,100	3,000	172%
China	3,250	7,000	115%
Taiwan	390	700	81%
Singapore	160	230	41%
Korea	960	1,200	25%

COUNTRY	CURRENT DOLLAR GDP	PPP GDP	IMPLIED DOLLAR UNDER VALUATION
Japan	4,400	4,300	−2%
Canada	1,450	1,250	−12%
Germany	3,300	2,800	−15%
Australia	900	760	−16%
United Kingdom	2,800	2,100	−23%
Switzerland	400	300	−29%

in 2000;[1] it has gone from a 15% overvaluation against European countries like Germany in 2000 to a 15% undervaluation in early 2008. The dollar is down 30% since 2000, but from an expensive starting point. When the dollar was overly expensive, it contributed to the growth of the U.S. trade deficit by making U.S. exports expensive everywhere in the world and by encouraging U.S. businesses such as Wal-Mart to buy foreign products that looked amazingly cheap compared with comparable products in the U.S.

The broadest perspective indicates that the dollar has merely returned to the level it held in 1994–95, before the massive rise in the dollar and resulting increase in the U.S. trade deficit. The dollar has even adjusted downward by a small amount against Asian currencies in recent years, though not enough. A bigger decline against Asian currencies would help U.S. businesses increase exports to Asia. On the IMF PPP, the dollar is still overvalued versus India at 170% of the PPP price today, but that's down from a 2000 overvaluation of 217%.

According to the IMF's calculation of how much goods and services a currency can purchase, an overvaluation of 217% means that a dollar in 2000 could buy more than twice the value of goods internationally as the equivalent amount of the Indian currency at the then prevailing rate of exchange. On a trade weighted basis, we are back to the 1994–95 level of the dollar. This can be seen on the chart of the Trade Weighted Dollar below, which evaluates the dollar against currencies, weighed according to each country's flow of trade with the U.S.[2]

Trade activity often responds to changes in exchange rates with a lag of many years. Changing trading partners can start with a long selling process, then it takes time to set up new contractual relationships followed by the work of increasing production to meet demand. Lastly, end user demand can take years to develop and grow. In 1994–95, the U.S. current account deficit was 1.5% of GDP. As the dollar appreciated

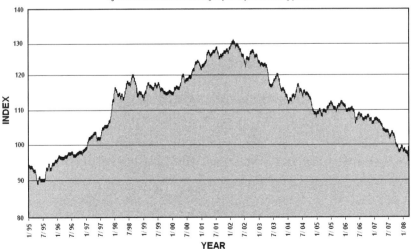

TRADE WEIGHTED DOLLAR
weighted average of the foreign exchange value of U.S. dollar
against the currencies of a broad group of major U.S. trading partners

40% over the next seven years, the current account deficit expanded to 4% of GDP. We are now seeing the same trend in reverse.

At this moment, trade is shifting back to favor U.S. products. In 2005 the Ex-Oil (excluding oil) Trade Deficit started to decline after increasing for years. It is responding to the weakening dollar. The weaker dollar adds to U.S. GDP growth by encouraging U.S. importers to substitute U.S. made products for foreign merchandise, and it encourages foreign companies to buy U.S. goods instead of buying products from outside the U.S. This is extremely good for U.S. GDP growth and jobs. The risk is that a weaker dollar can create inflation.

Weak Currencies and Inflation

A weak currency can be a problem if it creates inflation. That is the major concern for the U.S. Federal Reserve as it evaluates the fall in the dollar. If a country has no idle workers and no idle plants to produce more goods, a weak currency will provide companies the opportunity to raise prices. A weaker currency at home makes domestic goods and assets appear cheap to foreign buyers and investors. Increased demand from foreign buyers cannot practically be met with more goods if plants are already working at maximum capacity. Manufacturers will sell the output from their existing plants to the higher bid from foreign buyers, indirectly driving up prices in the country whose currency is falling.

If a country has excess workers available and idle plants ready to be put to work, a weaker currency will produce a new demand for goods that manufacturers can readily supply by hiring the unemployed and increasing the rate of plant utilization. So, in this case, extra demand does not lead to higher prices just faster growth.

As the dollar becomes weaker versus the Euro, European manufacturers find it more difficult to export to the U.S., but European consumers find American products available at a lower Euro currency price than was possible before. This increasing foreign demand is evident in quarterly U.S. GDP data. But as of June, 2008, there is no strong evidence that the weaker dollar is having a major influence on U.S. Consumer Price Inflation (CPI). The headline CPI has moved higher but the core rate, excluding food and energy, has been stable. So far, the weak dollar has not caused a major increase in most manufactured goods prices, indicating that the U.S. has sufficient excess capacity to absorb the switch from importing goods to producing more domestically. The recent increase in food and oil prices seems more related to demand outside the U.S. than to the value of the dollar.

Since the end of 2000, near the dollar's high, the Headline Consumer Price Index, a measure of inflation that examines the typical basket of goods purchased by the U.S. consumer, including food and energy, has moved up from 174 to a level of 211 (February 2008), an increase of less than 3% per year, even including the surge in oil and food prices.

Asian Currency Intervention

A number of countries, particularly Asian countries that are highly dependent on International trade for growth, have intervened heavily in foreign exchange markets. They have been busy buying dollars and selling their own currency. The result for these countries is that they are building up very large reserves of U.S. dollars at their central banks. In the last few years, Asian Central Banks have been trying to control the value of their currencies against the dollar. Not uniquely, but most notably, this was initiated by the Chinese central bank's decision to devalue their own currency, the Yuan, by 60%. After that happened in 1993, there were several years of tremendous turmoil in the Asian currency markets.

This was especially tough on Japan, South Korea, Singapore, and other Asian countries that were competing against China to export to the United States. Suddenly they found that China was undercutting them with artificially low prices, and the major Asian economies simply collapsed in the late 1990s, driven by their inability to compete in the U.S. with goods exported by China. Suddenly,

after the 1993 devaluation, Wal-Mart and every other discount chain
in this country went to China for their goods, because they were so
much cheaper.

But all the other countries that had been supplying the U.S. consumer up to that point were devastated. And it was the ripple effect
of that enormous change that led to the collapse of the Asian
economies in the late 1990s. Japan was hurt very badly, and it wasn't
until 2007 that Japan regained their 1995 level of manufacturing
production.

In almost every case these countries were also forced to undergo
huge devaluations against the dollar in order to be competitive against
the Chinese in selling manufactured goods to the U.S. The intervention by these countries' central banks was an effort to keep their own
currencies weak against the dollar.

	CHINA	MEXICO	RUSSIA	INDIA	BRAZIL
1994	5.7/dlr	6.2/dlr	2.5/dlr	31/dlr	.87/dlr
2002	8.3/dlr	11/dlr	33/dlr	49/dlr	3.5/dlr
2007	7.4/dlr	10.85/dlr	24/dlr	39/dlr	1.78/dlr
1994–2007					
Dollar change	+30%	+75%	+960%	+26%	+105%
1994 GDP	13.1%	4.4%	−12.7%	6.8%	5.9%
2001–07 GDP	10.1%	2.4%	6.3%	7.2%	3.1%

In each country a declining currency has helped in terms of domestic growth. Foreign sales growth drives higher domestic production as
well as employment: both desirable outcomes.

These countries, including all those listed in the chart above, have
been at the forefront of global growth in the developing world over the
last 10 years. Since 2001 the economies of these countries have grown
at an average pace of 7.7% per year. In turn, they are reinvesting that
growth heavily into new and better production facilities. These coun-

tries all massively lowered the value of their currencies during the 1990s as trade barriers came down and they joined in global trade agreements.[3] The risk for these countries is the potential for losses on the excess dollar balances they're currently holding.

Assessment

A weak, or inexpensive, currency isn't necessarily bad. If it were, why would the Asian countries be buying trillions of U.S. dollars to keep their own currencies weak? While the dollar has dropped considerably from 2001, its extremely overvalued level at that time was unsustainable and contributed directly to the increase in the U.S. trade deficit.

The recent weakening of the dollar has just returned it to the average exchange rates of the early 1990's. This makes U.S. merchandise less costly, which leads to increased exports. The last time exchange rates were at current levels, the result was a reduction of the U.S. trade deficit to only 1.5% of GDP. It is likely a return of the dollar to this more sustainable level will, as it did before, continue to lower the trade deficit and help keep U.S. GDP growth strong. The dollar is definitely not at an extreme level of weakness. There certainly is no dollar crisis. The U.S. dollar has simply returned to a sustainable level, closer to its long-term Purchasing Power Parity, according to the IMF.

The risk associated with an inexpensive dollar is that it could spur inflation as the manufacturing sector starts to push up against capacity limits to meet increasing demand for its products. As of June 2008 when this book went to press, while headline inflation, which includes food and energy, was trending upward, core inflation which excludes those items was not signaling signs of concern.

POTENTIAL LOSS TO NATIONAL GDP OF SUDDEN DOLLAR DEVALUATION

Taiwan	24.00%
China	15.00%
Russia	12.00%
India	9.00%
South Korea	9.00%
Brazil	5.00%

The buildup in Foreign Exchange Reserves by developing economies is the direct result of countries trying to maintain low "competitive" exchange rates for their own currencies to maximize export growth. As discussed earlier, for some of these countries the Foreign Exchange Currency Reserves represent a major percentage of the country's annual GDP. China went from insignificant foreign currency reserves to $1.6 trillion by January 2008. That is more than $1,000 per person in China. In 2007, China increased its dollar reserves by 43%. In 2007, India increased its reserves by 55% to $290 billion. At the same time, Russia has increased its reserves by 59% to $470 billion. Brazil has repaid its dollar debt and additionally built $168 billion in reserves.

Large excess foreign currency reserves is an imbalance that can be dangerous for countries holding large dollar reserves as a percent of their GDP, particularly if there were a major crisis of confidence in the U.S. or the U.S. dollar.[4] Such countries run a huge risk to their national net worth. The Foreign Exchange loss as a percent of GDP for countries holding large reserves—assuming reserves are primarily in U.S. dollars—of a 30% drop in the dollar is shown in the chart above. These losses are real because governments have to borrow domestically in their own currency to access funds to sell on international markets, in order to buy the dollars that go into their reserves.

If the dollar goes down, the domestic debt incurred by a foreign government to provide money to buy dollars must still be repaid in the now more expensive domestic (non U.S.) currency. The chart shows the potential real loss to each country's excessive foreign currency reserves, as a hit to the country's GDP, in the event of a sudden dollar devaluation. The U.S. economy is unlikely to suffer materially from a weaker dollar, however. A softer dollar is more likely to aid U.S. GDP growth by encouraging an expansion of exports. So long as our markets and international commerce remain strong, there is unlikely to be any sort of dollar crisis that could have anything more than a short-term impact on the U.S. economy.

II

Foreign Affairs

8

Iraq for the Rational

The angrier you are about the war in Iraq, the more this chapter is for you. Though we harbor no illusions that the facts presented here will change opinions about the war's worthiness, we hope to diminish the extreme anger which is usually rooted in false or incomplete information. Political and media pressure has intensified the war of words over the past four years almost as much as the war on the ground, and tempers run high on this issue. We believe that more knowledge can provide some measure of relief and a sense that the system is not actually as broken as those around the world have been led to believe.

Stabilizing Iraq's government, law enforcement, military, and civilian infrastructure so that U.S. forces can leave with confidence is obviously the main focus now. But eliminating false perceptions about the war is important as well. If the shallow view of the world held by the most cynical people were accurate, fears about a global superpower run amok as a result of failed checks and balances would be justified. We think more complete information reveals that this fear is unfounded. If this chapter helps to cause some readers to reconsider

their cynicism and hate, and to restore some faith in the American
process, it will have served its purpose.

CONVENTIONAL WISDOM

The U.S. is at war in Iraq because Bush and Cheney lied. False claims
about WMD got us into an unwinnable quagmire that was really
about oil.

Typical Headlines

"Truth Is the First Casualty; Is Credibility the Second?"
   —*New York Times, Jun. 8, 2003*

"Bush Wanted War"
   —*Washington Post, Mar. 30, 2006*

"Bush Led U.S. to War on 'False Pretenses'"
   —*MSNBC, Jan. 23, 2008*

Facts

Let's first keep in mind that the U.S. was already at war in Iraq prior
to the invasion, a fact amazingly few Americans seem to remember.
The U.S. and U.K. flew 280,000 sorties and dropped over 1,650
bombs on 385 Iraqi military sites during the Clinton administration.[1]
Just two days before September 11, U.S. fighter aircraft were firing at
military targets and being fired upon in the skies above Iraq. Six Iraqi
casualties were inflicted on that day.[2] In the early 1990's, well after
the end of the first gulf war, U.S. troops engaged Iraqi government
troops—within Iraq—and pushed them back from Iraq's northern
mountains to prevent the slaughter of thousands of Kurds.[3]

We should also not forget that "regime change" in Iraq became a
stated goal of United States foreign policy when the "Iraq Liberation
Act" was signed into law by Bill Clinton in January, 1998. The act

directed that: "It should be the policy of the United States to support efforts to remove the regime headed by Saddam Hussein from power in Iraq and to promote the emergence of a democratic government to replace that regime."

In the end, Saddam Hussein's government was removed because it failed to comply with (a) the treaty the Iraqi dictator signed after the First Gulf War in 1990, and then (b) the demands of eighteen U.N. Security Council resolutions.[4] One can not understand the case made for war and the related widely-publicized intelligence failures without some knowledge of the events that took place and the actions taken by the United Nations after the First Gulf War.

Working backward, the last U.N. Security Council resolution prior to invasion, Resolution 1441, was passed unanimously by all fifteen member nations, including France, Germany, Russia, and China, as well as Arab countries such as Syria. This was described at the time as the "final ultimatum" demanding that Iraq comply with the international mandates or face serious consequences.

The terms of the resolution declared this as "a final opportunity to comply with its disarmament obligations." Saddam Hussein understood the potential repercussions but did not comply. He thumbed his nose at the world community, and most of the delegates on the Security Council believed the time had come for "serious consequences."[5]

By that time the most severe of sanctions had already been applied to Iraq. There's no doubt they were causing serious hardships for Iraqis, but the Hussein regime refused to cooperate. Prior to the next U.N. vote—to actually commit to war under the U.N. banner—France and Russia signaled that they would not vote to invade. The reader can judge, after the facts are provided in Chapter 11, whether the U.N.'s Oil-for-Food scandal played a role in that decision. However, the U.S. and 48 other countries agreed that the time had come for action.

Here are the important sections from Resolution 1441, passed November 8, 2002, four and a half months prior to the coalition invasion of Iraq:

The United Nations Security Council Acting under Chapter VII of the Charter of the United Nations:

1. Decides that Iraq has been and remains in material breach of its obligations under relevant resolutions, including resolution 687 (1991), in particular through Iraq's failure to cooperate with United Nations inspectors and the IAEA, and to complete the actions required under paragraphs 8 to 13 of resolution 687 (1991) . . .

2. Decides that, in order to begin to comply with its disarmament obligations, in addition to submitting the required biannual declarations, the Government of Iraq shall provide to UNMOVIC [United Nations Monitoring, Verification, and Inspection Commission], the IAEA [International Atomic Energy Agency], and the Council, not later than 30 days from the date of this resolution, a currently accurate, full, and complete declaration of all aspects of its programmes to develop chemical, biological, and nuclear weapons, ballistic missiles, and other delivery systems such as unmanned aerial vehicles and dispersal systems designed for use on aircraft, including any holdings and precise locations of such weapons, components, sub-components, stocks of agents, and related material and equipment, the locations and work of its research, development and production facilities, as well as all other chemical, biological, and nuclear programmes, including any which it claims are for purposes not related to weapon production or material.[6]

Saddam Hussein's government did not comply with this United Nations ultimatum. Instead, the Iraqi ambassador provided a 1,200 page document in December 2002 that simply repeated previous incomplete declarations. U.N. weapons inspectors concluded that Iraq failed to account for substantial chemical and biological stockpiles which UNMOVIC had confirmed as existing as late as 1998.

In March of 2002, the chairman of the independent WMD Commission, Hans Blix, said that, "Iraq appears not to have come to a genuine acceptance—not even today—of the disarmament, which was demanded of it and which it needs to carry out to win the confidence of the world and to live in peace." Blix reported further that the Iraqi regime had allegedly misplaced 1,000 tons of VX nerve agent—one of the most toxic chemical agents ever developed.[7] Subsequent reports showed that an astonishing array of chemical and biological components, as well as armed munitions and SCUD missiles, had simply vanished and remained "unaccounted for."

There had never been any question that Saddam had WMD. He had used them repeatedly in the past, killing more than 5,000 Kurds in the brutal massacre at Halabja in 1988, and at least 182,000 murdered at Anfal the same year. Dozens of stories have been published in books and magazines detailing Iraq's use of these weapons.[8] There are videos on the Internet with heartrending pictures and testimony of how Saddam's thugs massacred innocent civilians with poisonous gasses.[9] You can also find videos of Saddam's opponents being thrown off the tops of buildings.

After the fall of Baghdad in 2003, more than 275 mass graves were discovered, each containing from fifty to several thousand bodies. Remains uncovered from those sites showed that many had been victims of chemical or biological weapons. Yet, when the search for WMD began in earnest at the end of the war, Saddam's stockpiles were nowhere to be found.

Key Terms

First Gulf War—The world was shocked when, on August 2, 1990, Iraqi tanks, aircraft, and infantry, on orders from Saddam Hussein, invaded and brutalized the tiny nation of Kuwait. Following the invasion, the U.N. Security Council passed 12 resolutions condemning the assault and giving Iraq until January 15, 1991 to withdraw. When Saddam defiantly refused, a 30-nation coalition led by the U.S. entered the region to expel Iraq's forces, destroying most of that country's military with high-precision weapons delivered by aircraft, missiles, and rockets.[10] Television coverage of Operation Desert Storm gave the world an unprecedented view of the aerial war in real time.

The ground war, which began February 23, lasted exactly 100 hours. The rape and devastation Saddam's military had perpetrated on their Arab neighbors was tragic. Thousands of civilians were dead or gravely injured, the Kuwaiti countryside was littered with land mines, and more than 700 oil wells had been deliberately set ablaze on Saddam's orders, massively destroying animal and plant life in the region. Kuwaiti citizens praised their deliverers, but the stories of massacres and atrocities were chilling. The U S. Corps of Engineers and foreign contractors actively assisted in the reconstruction of Kuwait, the cost of which, according to Kuwaiti sources, would top $700 billion.

IAEA—The International Atomic Energy Agency is a United Nations commission headquartered in Vienna. The IAEA sets standards for acquisition and use of nuclear materials and conducts inspections to ensure the peaceful use of nuclear power and safeguard public health. The agency administers the Treaty on the Non-Proliferation of Nuclear Weapons (NPT), which requires international cooperation and a system for monitoring energy development plans. IAEA inspectors are authorized to monitor transport of weapons-grade nuclear fuel to ensure that none is diverted for military use.

UNMOVIC—The United Nations Monitoring, Verification, and Inspection Commission was created in December 1999 by U.N. Resolution 1284. UNMOVIC, the successor of the U.N. Special

Commission, UNSCOM, was authorized to verify destruction of Iraq's chemical and biological weapons, and missiles with a range of more than 150 kilometers. Under order from Saddam, Iraqi scientists and engineers successfully hid munitions and other WMD from inspectors, which ultimately became the real reason for the invasion of Iraq in 2003. UNMOVIC inspectors left Iraq in March 2003, but the commission continued to operate outside the country with a roster of more than 300 experts in weapons detection. The commission's mandate was eventually terminated in June 2007 by Security Council Resolution 1762.

WMD—Weapons of Mass Destruction (WMD) are those which can kill large numbers of humans and cause large-scale damage to buildings and infrastructure. The most commons types are nuclear, biological, and chemical weapons, but WMD may also include other types of non-conventional weapons. In military shorthand, the term ABC refers to atomic, biological, and chemical weapons; NBC refers to nuclear, biological, and chemical weapons, and CBRN refers to chemical, biological, radiological, and nuclear weapons.

Oil-for-Food Program—Under the UN sanctions imposed during the early-nineties, the international community agreed not to buy oil from Iraq until the country complied with U.N. resolution requirements. The Oil-for-Food program was established in April 1995 by Security Council Resolution 986. The purpose was to allow Iraq to sell oil to bona fide traders in exchange for food and other humanitarian necessities, to soften the impact of U.N. sanctions on Iraqi citizens. Between 1997 and 2002, until revelations of the scope of Saddam's double-dealing erupted in a major scandal, Iraq sold more than $67 billion in oil and issued $38 billion in letters of credit to purchase goods and commodities.[11]

Most of that revenue, unfortunately, ended up in Saddam's possession or was transferred to private bank accounts in Europe and the Middle East. The program ended in November 2003 with Security Council Resolution 1483, which lifted civilian sanctions on Iraq and provided for termination of the program. Oversight was then transferred to the Coalition Provisional Authority and any remaining funds were given to the Iraqi Development Fund. We offer a fuller treatment of this issue in Chapter 11.

Assessment

Many around the world are passionately opposed to the war in Iraq without even knowing what led to it. While some downplay the importance of resolution 1441—or ignore it—one can NOT understand the rationale for war without it. Since under this resolution Saddam could have avoided an impending disaster by simply telling the U.N. what had been done with his WMD, it was almost universally assumed that the reason he was not doing so was that he still had them. This universal assumption established the context for those assessing—and reporting on—Iraq's WMD capabilities over the following 4-plus months leading up to the invasion. The claims of WMD were bold because those making them had what they believed was irrefutable logic on their side.

Much has been made of the failure of the intelligence community and also the failure of the press to push back on the bold claims being made about the existence of WMD. Whether you believe that Saddam actually had WMD or not, whether or not you view resolution 1441 as an important geopolitical event or not, you must acknowledge that it affected the context importantly, paving the way for reporters and policymakers to make assertions that were unusually bold given the relative lack of complete information. Apparently it's easy to forget an old context when things get heated.

Some might think that requiring Saddam Hussein to provide evidence that he had destroyed something that had been destroyed is doubletalk. This lacks an understanding of the nature of the weapons he had. There were large confirmed stockpiles of lethal, horribly dangerous weapons, some of which were used against Iran and on Iraqi citizens. These weapons could not have been destroyed without leaving many memories of the destruction process and probably many written records. If the WMD were In fact destroyed, a few conversations with those responsible for their destruction or disarmament could have settled the matter and avoided the mess.

Saddam apologists have explained this by saying that he actually believed he still had WMD because his officers were afraid to tell him that the weapons had all been used, destroyed, or perhaps never existed. Those with this line of thinking typically also hold that the world leaders and press is at fault for not knowing something that Saddam didn't know himself, and something that also contradicted statements made by the CIA and intelligence agencies around the world.

CONVENTIONAL WISDOM

George Bush made the case for war solely on the WMD claim and then changed it later to spreading freedom through a democratic Iraq.

Typical Headlines

"Report: No WMD Stockpiles in Iraq"
    —*CNN, Oct. 7, 2004*

"Carnegie Group says Bush Made Wrong Claims on WMD"
    —*The Guardian, Jan. 8 2004*

"Bush Pledges to Spread Freedom:
Global Focus on Rights Would Be a Shift in Policy"
    —*Washington Post, Jan. 21, 2005*

Facts

During his address to the nation one week prior to full-scale invasion of Iraq, President Bush made it clear that the U.S. was acting in concert with the wishes of the world community. In the first paragraph of that address, Mr. Bush confirmed that the emphasis had shifted from international concerns about the physical presence of WMD in Iraq to the Iraqi government's failure to report on the disposition of WMD. He says in his opening remarks:

> My fellow citizens, events in Iraq have now reached the final days of decision. For more than a decade, the United States and other nations have pursued patient and honorable efforts to disarm the Iraqi regime without war. *That regime pledged to reveal and destroy all of its weapons of mass destruction as a condition for ending the Persian Gulf War in 1991.*
>
> Since then, the world has engaged in twelve years of diplomacy. We have passed more than a dozen resolutions in the United Nations Security Council. We have sent hundreds of weapons inspectors to oversee the disarmament of Iraq.
>
> Our good faith has not been returned. The Iraqi regime has used diplomacy as a ploy to gain time and advantage. *It has uniformly defied Security Council resolutions* . . . (emphasis added).

Near the end of his remarks, the President laid out the vision for democracy:

> Unlike Saddam Hussein, we believe the Iraqi people are deserving and capable of human liberty, and when the dictator has departed, they can set an example to all the Middle East of a vital and peaceful and self-governing nation.
>
> The United States, with other countries, will work to advance liberty and peace in that region.

Related to the specific claim that "Bush lied," consider the following. The three most frequently cited events are:

1. George Tenet, head of the CIA, told George Bush two weeks prior to invasion that it was a "slam dunk case" that Saddam Hussein had WMD.

2. Colin Powell delivered a speech to the U.N. in February 2002 in which many claims were made that turned out to be false. Before going before the U.N. with this information, however, Powell sat face to face with George Tenet and asked for assurance that all of the facts he would present were unassailable. It turned out that many could not be proven after the invasion.

3. George W. Bush, in his January 2003 State of the Union Address, made the now famous sixteen-word claim: "The British Government has learned that Saddam Hussein recently sought significant quantities of uranium from Africa." This claim was supposedly discredited by former Ambassador Joe Wilson after a trip to Niger to investigate the claim for the CIA. Later investigation by the CIA and the media showed that Wilson's report did not dispel a false rumor but actually tended to confirm that agents of Saddam Hussein had, in fact, traveled to meet with industry officials in Niger in 1999, where they undoubtedly discussed the country's only valuable export, yellowcake uranium, which is a low-grade precursor of nuclear fuel.[12]

Regarding points 1 and 2: George Tenet was appointed to his position as head of the CIA by Bill Clinton, not George Bush. His claims were possibly false, but the source was *not* the Bush administration. Regarding point 3: While the Bush administration later said the infamous sixteen words should not have been included in the State of the Union speech, it is nevertheless true that (a) the British did inform the CIA of the meeting in Niger between agents of that country's government and emissaries from Iraq; (b) the British government later issued a statement affirming that they stood by the claim; and (c) a special panel investigation by the U.S. Senate also confirmed that the sixteen-word statement was probably true.

The fact that Resolution 1441 went to a unanimous vote of its fifteen members is sufficient evidence to prove that the Bush administration was not acting alone in the belief that Iraq had WMD. Without such a belief, the resolution would have been absurd. Further, the following quotes indicate that almost all world leaders at the time believed that Iraq had WMD:

Public Statements about Saddam's WMDs

The following public officials, many of whom now claim the war in Iraq is illegitimate, made public statements during the run-up to war indicating that they believed that Iraq had chemical and biological weapons, and an active program of nuclear weapons development:

> "People can quarrel with whether we should have more troops in Afghanistan or internationalize Iraq, or whatever, but it is incontestable that on the day I left office, there were unaccounted for stocks of biological and chemical weapons."
> —*President Bill Clinton, July, 22, 2003*[13]

> "Iraq is a long way from [here], but what happens there matters a great deal here. For the risks that the leaders of a rogue state will use nuclear, chemical or biological weapons against us or our allies is the greatest security threat we face."
> —*Secretary of State Madeline Albright, Feb. 18, 1998.*

> "Saddam Hussein has been engaged in the development of weapons of mass destruction technology which is a threat to countries in the region and he has made a mockery of the weapons inspection process."
> —*Rep. Nancy Pelosi (D, CA), Dec. 16, 1998.*

"We know that he has stored secret supplies of biological and chemical weapons throughout his country."
—*Vice President Al Gore, Sept. 23, 2002.*

"I will be voting to give the President of the United States the authority to use force—if necessary—to disarm Saddam Hussein because I believe that a deadly arsenal of weapons of mass destruction in his hands is a real and grave threat to our security."
—*Sen. John F. Kerry (D, MA), Oct. 9, 2002.*

"In the four years since the inspectors left, intelligence reports show that Saddam Hussein has worked to rebuild his chemical and biological weapons stock, his missile delivery capability, and his nuclear program. He has also given aid, comfort, and sanctuary to terrorists, including al-Qaeda members. It is clear, however, that if left unchecked, Saddam Hussein will continue to increase his capacity to wage biological and chemical warfare, and will keep trying to develop nuclear weapons."
—*Sen. Hillary Clinton (D, NY), Oct. 10, 2002*

In an article, in the Wall Street Journal, former Clinton CIA director James Woolsey made several points—that Saddam possibly intentionally misled the world into thinking he still possessed WMD to keep his status as a power player in the region; that stockpiles of WMD possibly remained only to be destroyed at the last minute; that WMD-related material "probably" entered Syria months before the war; that Iraq admitted making 8,500 liters (8.5 tons) of anthrax, which if reduced to powder, could fill a dozen easily portable suitcases; and that "Iraq's ties with terrorist groups in the '90s are clear," with a decade worth of connections between Iraq and al-Qaida, "including training in poisons, gases, and explosives."

Weapons hunter David Kay, testifying before the Senate Armed Services Committee, said that based on the pre-war intelligence, Saddam Hussein posed "a gathering, serious threat to the world." Hussein's scientists possibly misled the former dictator into believing Iraq possessed WMD, with the scientists possibly misappropriating funds. Though he also said "we were all wrong" regarding WMD in Iraq, which was widely publicized, he also said that, based on his investigation, Iraq was "far more dangerous than even we anticipated."

The bipartisan Silberman-Robb commission and Senate Intelligence Committees both scrutinized the claims made by the intelligence community and the justification for war. Both concluded that "every intelligence agency believed that Saddam's regime had weapons of mass destruction." They concluded that no one lied.[14]

The post invasion Duelfer report concluded the following: "Hussein maintained the capability to produce them [WMD] on short notice. There was abundant evidence of contacts between Saddam's regime and al Qaeda and other terrorist groups. Given Saddam's hostility to the United States and his stonewalling of the United Nations, American leaders had every reason to believe he posed a grave threat. Removing him removed that threat."[15]

There was never any question that Saddam Hussein was a brutal tyrant who would stop at nothing to achieve his goals. The record of his atrocities was growing day by day. Right up to the moment coalition forces entered Iraq, the overwhelming majority of world leaders agreed that, whether by diplomacy or by force, the Iraqi dictator had to be removed. When the U.S.-led coalition invaded, in March 2003, the potential use of WMD by Iraq against our forces was listed by Defense Secretary Donald Rumsfeld and senior commanders on the ground as their "Number One Concern," and was the focus of much of the military preparations. Who will forget the images of American soldiers, covered head to toe in specialized gear and face masks in the 100-degree heat, because of the presumed risk of a chemical weapons strike by Iraqi forces?

Assessment

Lying, by any reasonable definition, involves the intent to deceive. Clearly President George Bush and General Colin Powell believed that Saddam Hussein had WMD. Their claims were based on information delivered to the administration by others who had no partisan reason to make false claims. Their military plans were based on thoughtful consideration of the context, evidence, and current events, and by the terms of U.N. Resolution 1441.

Even if some of the facts had later been shown to be incorrect, the president and his advisers did not lie. However, those who continue to repeat the "Bush lied" mantra—knowing the claim is disingenuous—actually do fit the "intent to deceive" requirement.

The premise of the U.S. and coalition invasion of Iraq was not: "We're going to invade Iraq because we know they have WMD." Rather, it was almost the opposite. The premise was: "We're going to invade because we don't know if they still have WMD, (more precisely, he has been required to tell us what he did with them and has refused) and Saddam Hussein is a tyrant who can't be trusted." We knew without a doubt that Iraq had WMD at one time, that the international weapons inspectors were being blocked by Saddam, and that Saddam's regime refused to provide the accounting of their weapons and weapons-related technologies as required by resolutions of the international community.

WMD: Where Are They Now?

Since the end of Operation Desert Storm, many credible sources have reported that there are at least three facilities in Syria currently producing chemical weapons, near the cities of Damascus, Hama, and Safira (in the Aleppo area). A senior Syrian journalist has reported that Iraq's WMD were transported to Syria prior to the U.S. invasion, and were hidden in three bunker complexes in that country.[16] In addition, the testimony of a former high-ranking Iraqi Air Force officer published in this country after the U.S. invasion describes in detail how and when

WMD were ferried out of Iraq and into Syria, in fifty-six sorties using retrofitted 747 and 727 aircraft, by civilian commercial pilots carrying out Saddam's direct orders.[17]

Additional support for these reports comes from former members of the Iraq Study Group (ISG) who found evidence of hidden stockpiles in Southern Iraq but were rebuffed by their superiors, who refused to authorize recovery operations. Former ISG inspector Bill Tierney, who speaks and reads Arabic fluently, made headlines in 2005 and 2006 when he translated twelve hours of conversation from audio tapes of General Staff meetings, in which Saddam and top-level aides (including Ambassador Tariq Aziz) discussed Iraq's use of chemical weapons and how the Iraqis had successfully misled U.N. weapons inspectors.

Assessment—The Courage to Act

Did the U.S. government really assemble a thirty-nation coalition and commit its military and diplomatic resources to war in Iraq because Bush lied? The assumption is unreasonable, but if you believe it's true, ask yourself this question: Should the U.S. and the UK—after eighteen United Nations resolutions and twelve years of arrogant defiance by Saddam Hussein—have pushed for the "final ultimatum" requiring Iraq to provide an accounting of their WMD programs? Or should the U.N. have said, "Never mind. Let's just continue with this costly containment, punishing Iraqi civilians with sanctions and a corrupt Oil-for-Food program."? And all those previous resolutions? Should we simply have ignored them as well?

If Resolution 1441 had passed and no serious actions were taken, the U.N. Security Council might as well have shut down, having completely destroyed the credibility of the U.S., the UK, and the Security Council itself. On the other hand, by taking action the coalition ensured that when the U.N. votes similarly in the future, there will be a credible threat of action, not empty resolutions that will drag on forever with no real threat of force behind them.

A leader's job often involves making decisions with imperfect or incomplete information, and then advocating for the action required. Waiting for perfect information is almost always a recipe for disaster, and leaders worth their salt don't put things in motion by saying, "Well, we think he's dangerous, but we're not totally sure about that, and maybe we should just wait and see."

By the same token, the idea that the Iraq War was only about oil is disingenuous and ill-informed. The decision to invade Iraq was "about oil" only to the extent that it was the vast supply of oil in that country that enabled the Tyrant of Baghdad to pursue his maniacal lust for power for more than three decades.

CONVENTIONAL WISDOM

Democracy and Islam are incompatible. There's no point in trying to establish a democratic state in the Middle East. They'll never accept it.

Typical Headlines

"Is It Possible to Give Primacy to Sharia Law and Still Have a Democratic Society?"
    —*PBS "Wide Angle," July 2003*

"Democracy and Islamic Law Don't Mix"
    —*CNSNews.com, Apr. 10, 2006*

"Most Iraqis Favor Immediate U.S. Pullout, Poll Shows"
    —*Washington Post, Sept. 2006*

Facts

The leading Shiite cleric in Iraq, Grand Ayatollah Ali al-Sistani, believes Islam and democracy are compatible.[18] More than 70% of the mostly Muslim citizens of Iraq voted in their first elections, in January 2005, despite significant risk to life and limb, indicating that they believe they are compatible. Here's how they expressed their views in the new Iraqi constitution:

> 1st—Islam is the official religion of the state and is a basic source of legislation:
> (a) No law can be passed that contradicts the undisputed rules of Islam.
> (b) No law can be passed that contradicts the principles of Democracy.
> (c) No law can be passed that contradicts the rights and basic freedoms outlined in this Constitution.

Assessment

Those who think Islam and democracy are incompatible are at odds with some important stakeholders. These people are (a) Muslims, and (b) citizens of Iraq. We believe their opinions carry more weight than those of the American media elite or the public intellectuals. There are, in fact, many intellectuals who do recognize the importance of a winning strategy in that country.

Kenneth M. Pollack, a Middle East scholar at the liberal Brookings Institution in Washington, wrote in a 2005 editorial in the *New York Times* that, "critics of the president who make parallels between Iraq and Vietnam are equally wrong. Iraq is far more important. Because of its oil wealth, its location in the most politically fragile region of the world, and its importance in the eyes of Arab nations that wonder if democracy is possible for them too, Iraq is critical to American interests in a way that Vietnam never was."[19]

Pollack's criticism of the Defense Department strategy in Iraq was the lack of an effective counterinsurgency plan, a reality that was eventually resolved in 2007 with the military Surge directed by General David Petraeus. But the belief that democracy can survive and thrive in that ancient country is a gamble well worth taking.

CONVENTIONAL WISDOM

Saddam was not a threat. We should have just left him alone.

Typical Headlines

"Carter: Iraq Threat Does Not Justify War"
    —*CNN, Jan. 2003*

"We Are Not 'A Nation In Danger'"
    —*CBS News, Aug. 5, 2004*

"Putin Slams U.S. for 'Pointless' Iraq War"
    —*CBS News, Oct. 18, 2007*

Facts

Was Saddam Hussein a legitimate threat to America and the world? Consider the following:

1. Saddam was publicly offering to pay $25,000 to the families of suicide bombers in Israel.[20]
2. The U.S. was Saddam Hussein's most hated enemy. The doormat of the Al-Rashid Hotel in Baghdad featured a mosaic of George H. W. Bush—the U.S. president who defeated Saddam in the First Gulf War—so that hotel guests could insult America with every step.[21]
3. Saddam moved as much as $40 billion of Iraq's oil wealth out of the country to his private bank accounts in Europe and the Persian Gulf states.[22]
4. Stockpiles of up to a million tons of conventional explosives were found around the country after the U.S. invasion. In addition, weapons inspectors David Kay,[23] Dave Gaubatz,[24] Bill Tierney,[25] and others have reported that Saddam ferried WMD

into Syria during the lead-up to the March 2003 invasion. This has been corroborated more recently by Iraqi journalists,[26] military officers,[27] research scientists,[28] and covert informants.

Assessment

Connect the dots. Given his hatred for America, the billions he stole from his own people, his long-term record of support for terrorism, and his record of torture, rape, and murder of political opponents, what are the odds that everything would have been just fine if Saddam had been left alone? What do you think Saddam's one million tons of explosives were for?

Refusing to acknowledge that evil tyrants really do exist is simply wishful thinking. We only need to remember the name Neville Chamberlain—the British prime minister who made concession to try and keep peace with Adolf Hitler until it was too late to avoid World War II—to see where that sort of naiveté can lead. Looking the other way, hoping the bad guys will just be nice and go away, has gotten countless nations into trouble throughout history.

CONVENTIONAL WISDOM

The war has been a disaster because there was no plan to follow up on the invasion in Iraq.

Typical Headlines

"Iraq War 'Disaster for Mid-East'"
    —*BBC News, Sept. 14, 2006*

"Ex-Commander in Iraq Faults War Strategy"
    —*Washington Post, Oct. 13, 2007*

"Mission Still Not Accomplished"
    —*New York Times, Mar. 20, 2008*

Facts

1. Major military operations were completed in twenty-one days with loss of life that was extremely low by historical standards.[29]

2. Most Iraqis welcomed the U.S. and coalition soldiers as liberators. American soldiers were met with flowers, until small groups of insurgents began firing weapons and blowing themselves up.

3. A provisional government was elected by the people.

4. A constitution was written by the people.

5. The constitution was approved and ratified by the people.

6. A new President, Prime Minister, and Parliament were elected.

Assessment

The creation of local and provisional governments, a national constitution, and national elections was an enormous undertaking under dangerous and difficult circumstances. None of that could have happened without a plan. We owe an enormous debt to the public servants and soldiers who risked their lives to do this difficult work on our behalf, and on behalf of the Iraqi people.

Yes, mistakes were made, as in any complex endeavor, and critical time was lost when the original plan had to be changed in response to unexpected developments on the ground. During the protracted time it took to assemble a provisional government, to create the institutions of democracy, write a constitution that would be seen as legitimate by all factions of that religiously divided nation, the insurgents sensed a growing lack of support for coalition efforts. That breakdown of support was clearly visible in the headlines of our own daily newspapers and international news broadcasts. The insurgents took this as encouragement that they might be able to force the foreigners to leave and, thus, to bring about the failure of the new government in Baghdad. Their mistake was that they didn't understand the resolve and resourcefulness of the American armed forces and diplomats.

Why didn't the world community support these efforts? Some were apparently afraid that a U.S. success in Iraq would encourage ever more imperialistic ventures from an out-of-control superpower whose leaders could justify invading other countries without international consensus. This fear would be justified if it were based on facts. But keeping in mind that Iraq's government (a) had already invaded Kuwait, (b) refused to comply with the treaty Saddam had signed at the end of that war and ten years of U.N. resolutions, (c) had used WMD on it own people and on civilians in the war with Iran, and (d) caused unimaginable suffering to their own people, the intervention by U.S.-led forces was a good idea which helped to ensure that circumstances like those would never again be repeated anywhere on earth.

Secondly, anger toward George Bush's "team," the Republican Party, was unprecedented as a result of an unusually divisive election and its ambiguous outcome in 2000. This anger led many in the other party to watch for, and even hope for, failure in Iraq. Selective perception can wield a powerful influence. Third, outside the U.S. there had been an ever-increasing buildup of anger toward the U.S., especially in Muslim countries, resulting from a sense of cultural intrusion. At the same time, envy of America's success, affluence, and world influence also plays a role in accelerating anger abroad, despite the fact that record numbers of people from all over the world are eager to pick up stakes and move to this country.

Lastly, "War is hell," always was, and always is polarizing. When casualties mount, people tend to buckle under the emotional pressure and become negative. But this doesn't necessarily mean the effort was unwarranted. Policemen are killed every day in the line of duty, but we're not asking for police officers to be withdrawn from our streets.

These and other factors have combined to create an irrational lack of support for what would otherwise have been seen as a noble cause. Wars are complex and notoriously full of errors of all kinds. This one has not been an exception. Reasonable people can disagree on whether the war has been "worth it." The cost in dollars and lives significantly exceeded expectations, and we may not know the outcome for years. It would be impossible, though, to make a credible argument that, having come this far, the world would be better for either Iraqis or Americans if the U.S. were to abruptly withdraw before Iraq is stabilized.

With success comes the possibility of a solution to problems that have eluded the Western world for centuries. If a successful democracy emerges in Iraq—even if it takes a decade or longer, as it did in the founding of this country—others are likely to follow, and the anger of Islamic extremists will be transformed into the pursuit of a better life throughout the Arab world.

What's Really at Stake Here?

"The stakes—for the United States and for the world—are enormous. Iraq lies in the center of a region critical to the well-being of the global system. It is surrounded by states intensely concerned about the nature and future of that country and its government. A failed Iraq could be a catastrophe for the Middle East and a calamity for the world. At the moment such an outcome would be inevitable without the U.S. presence."
—*Brent Scowcroft, Washington Post, Jan. 16, 2006*

CONVENTIONAL WISDOM

The U.S. rarely goes to war; but when we do the results are usually a disaster, as with Vietnam and Iraq; and the U.S. is hated for it.

Typical Headlines

"American Attitudes on Iraq Similar to Vietnam Era"
—*USA Today, Nov. 15, 2005*

"Only Hatred of U.S. Unites Iraq"
—*Seattle Post-Intelligencer, Dec. 11, 2007*

"Democrat Blames Iraq for Weak Economy"
—*AP, Apr. 12, 2008*

Facts

While there are individuals on both sides who oppose military engagement, in most cases the residents of the countries where the United States has been engaged appreciate the U.S. for resisting tyranny and oppression and promoting democracy and freedom. In particular, the people of these nations give high praise to the courage, competence, and compassion of our American soldiers, sailors, and airmen.

World War II was the last war fought by the United States in which the president asked Congress for a declaration of war. Since then, United States armed forces have been engaged in combat operations 13 times, in Korea (1950–53), Cuba (1961), Vietnam (1961–72), Dominican Republic (1965), Lebanon U.N. peacekeeping mission (1982), Grenada (1983), Panama (1989), the First Gulf War (1991), Somalia (1993), Haiti (1994), Bosnia (1994–95), Afghanistan (2001), and Iraq (2003–Present).[30]

America's record of success is unparalleled, yet we have never fought for land or treasure or hegemony over any other nation. Our aims since colonial times have been to foster freedom and independence at home and abroad, and to prevent the hopes of free people from being crushed under the iron heel of tyrants and dictators. Furthermore, the American economy, as we have already shown in these pages, is booming, and our influence around the world has never been greater. A dip in the market or short-term mortgage crisis will only stimulate new growth in the months ahead.

In a 2005 address in Little Rock, Arkansas, President Bush expressed this vision, saying:

> "I think the freest nation on the face of the earth has a duty to help those who desire and long for freedom to achieve that dream. And in so doing, this world of ours will be more peaceful, and Iraq will continue to stand with us."
> —*President George W. Bush, Feb. 4, 2005*

Assessment

There were many in this country who say the U.S. has no business fighting for the freedom of another country. The internal affairs of one country, they reasoned, are no business of another. We ought to be thankful that France didn't take that position in 1776 when they were petitioned to help the American colonists in their efforts to win their freedom from the British Empire. The American experiment in democracy would have been dead before it started without the help of French financial and military support.

When the U.S.-led coalition entered Iraq in March 2003, they did so, in part, at the request of the thousands of Iraqis who were calling for an end to Saddam Hussein's tyrannical regime. It would have been impossible to assemble and field their own militia: the punishment for suspected opposition of the tyrant was watching your wife and/or daughters being raped in Saddam's rape rooms, which were housed in the local police stations throughout Iraq.

To learn more about the amazing work done by American soldiers and civil servants on your behalf under the most difficult of conditions, we highly recommend Paul Bremer's powerful book, *My Year in Iraq*.[31]

9

Afghanistan: Showing the Way

CONVENTIONAL WISDOM

The effort in Afghanistan is worthy, but results have been poor and the coalition is cracking.

Typical Headlines

"Afghanistan Five Years Later: Poverty, Violence, Misery"
—*AP, Oct. 7, 2006*

"Stumbling in Afghanistan"
—*Washington Post, Mar. 3, 2006*

"Cracks in Coalition as Afghanistan Campaign Drags On"
—*The Guardian, Oct. 25, 2007*

Facts

A coalition led by NATO forces went into Afghanistan less than one month after the September 11 terrorist attacks in New York and Washington, DC. The purpose was to remove the brutal and repressive

Taliban regime that was harboring al-Qaeda and their terrorist training camps. The military victory was swift and decisive. Of the 41,000 troops deployed there, about half were American; the other half were from the forty coalition countries that supported the effort.

As of early 2008, there are still pockets of resistance, and problems existed in some of the remote mountainous regions of the country, but the accomplishments of the coalition effort in that country are impressive. A report by our Canadian partners in the reconstruction effort, summarized the progress as follows:

A population of 26 million Afghans are now free from the Taliban and 4.6 million refugees have returned to Afghanistan. In addition to establishing a credible government through two national elections (parliamentary and presidential), in which 10 million Afghans voted—41% of which were women—and an impressive 14,000 community district councils have been elected.

The lives of many Afghans have been immeasurably improved. Per capita income has doubled and Afghanistan's GDP has tripled. 200,000 Afghans, 90% of whom were women, have received microfinance business loans.

At least 7.2 million children have been vaccinated against polio; and 4.3 million vaccinated against common childhood diseases. 77% of Afghans have access to medical facilities—compared to less than 10% in 2001.

School attendance is up almost ten fold to 6 million children. One third of these students are girls, compared with no girls in 2001. 363,000 teachers have been provided with teaching material. Hygiene education has been provided to 3.4 million people.

In addition, the coalition has made much progress in improving the country's infrastructure. 3,000 miles of new and refurbished roads have been completed; 2,500 villages have electricity for the first time; 8,000 construction projects have been completed and 14,000 more are underway; 1,700 water reservoirs have been built; 130 agriculture projects, benefiting 300,000 farmers, have been started; 8,100 new water points and 8,000 latrine blocks, benefiting 3 million people, have been constructed; and 4,000 houses and shelters have been built for the needy.

Afghans are also more secure than before. 60,000 Taliban soldiers were disarmed and demobilized while 30,000 Afghan National Army soldiers and 46,000 Afghan National Police have been trained and equipped. 190,000 mines defused and removed.

Despite claims that the coalition was about to fall apart in late 2007, Germany, France, Canada, Australia, and New Zealand all reaffirmed their commitment to stay the course in Afghanistan, for "as long as it takes," or "at least through 2011." And in some cases, troop strength is actually increasing. Likewise, the General Secretary of the United Nations, Ban Ki-moon, made a similar pledge of ongoing support for the government in Kabul during a summit meeting on the future of NATO in Europe in April 2008.[1]

Assessment

The improvements in Afghanistan—none of which would have been possible under the repressive, cruel, and dangerous Taliban regime—are an inspiring demonstration of broad, unified global community in action. The effort was led by the United States. When the global press was trying to portray it as a failure, it was always the "U.S. led coalition." Now that it has succeeded, let's continue to call it what it was. It was led by the United States of America. To the many other countries who have done their part, we owe a deep appreciation.

CONVENTIONAL WISDOM

The Afghan people are bitterly divided. Most prefer the Taliban and their Islamic customs to the plans being imposed by the U.S. and NATO.

Typical Headlines

"Afghans' Uneasy Peace with Democracy"
—*Washington Post, Apr. 2006*

"More Afghans Support Taliban, Criticize U.S."
    —*Pravda, Dec. 2007*

"NATO Faces Afghanistan 'Problems'"
    —*BBC, July 2007*

Facts

Since coalition and Northern Alliance forces ousted the Taliban from the capital of Afghanistan in November 2001, the government has undergone a critical transformation. Al-Qaeda has lost its safe haven, a new democratic government was established, and on December 7, 2004, the citizens of that country elected Hamid Karzai as their president. Looking back at the progress that had been made, a 2006 report from the Pakistan News Service offered the following assessments of Democracy, Equality, Health Care, Education, and the Afghan Economy.

Progress in Afghanistan

Democracy: Prior to 2001 there was no national government and no democracy in Afghanistan. Today, however, Afghanistan has held a series of successful elections, and has a constitution, an elected president, and a parliament.

Equality: Women, banished from society under the Taliban, now have places in government. Eighty-seven women, 25% of the total number of the members of parliament, sit on the National Assembly. In addition, approximately 40% of Afghan children in schools today are girls—up from zero at the time of the NATO invasion.

Health care: Fully 80% of the Afghan population now has access to health care—up 10 times from 2001. For a country at Afghanistan's stage of development, this is extremely high.[*]

---

[*] Note that this estimate of access to medical care differs slightly from figures cited earlier by the Kandahar Reconstruction Team, but still represents a very impressive improvement.

Education: Almost 6 million Afghan children are in school today—six times more than 2001. University enrollment is up 10 times higher than in 2001, to more than 40,000 graduate and undergraduate students. Despite an increase of attacks by the Taliban, killing schoolteachers and burning down village schools, more than 1,000 schools were built or opened for the first time in the year 2006 alone.

Economy: The Afghan economy has tripled in national GDP since 2001, and per capita income has doubled. People simply have more money in their pocket, and the atmosphere in the major cities is enthusiastic and optimistic. After 25 years of war, the economy was almost non-existent. There was no centralized government to institute economic policy, and little infrastructure—not even a formal banking system. What commerce there was existed outside of any domestic or international structure. And there were few opportunities for Afghans to improve their lives.

Another important indicator of progress, the report concluded, is the fact that record numbers of Afghans who fled the country at the beginning of the war are now coming home. At the time of this report, more than four million refugees had returned to their native land—one of the largest return movements in history. They've come because they feel safer now, and feel they have a chance to build a better life for their families. A survey of Afghans across the country in 2006 found that 84% of the people consider themselves better off today than they were under the Taliban, and 76% said they feel security is better today than at any time in the last 25 years.[2]

Assessment

How do you measure success? A September 2006 Defense Department report offers insightful analysis of what has been going on in Afghanistan since operations began in that country. Before the events of September 11, al-Qaeda was in Afghanistan training thousands of would-be terrorists and planning attacks without restraint. At that time, the Taliban provided safe haven for terrorists and imposed a totalitarian religious regime on the entire Afghan population. Today that country is no longer a safe haven for al-Qaeda, and there are no functioning al-Qaeda training camps.

As peace is being restored in that devastated region, Afghanistan is becoming a strong partner in the ongoing War on Terror. The Afghan people are free of totalitarian leadership and are being led by democratically elected officials, including a president, a national assembly, and a new constitution. As a result of concerted international efforts, key al-Qaeda leaders have been killed, captured, or put on the run. The report then goes on to list the following accomplishments:

As Mujahedeen forces and the remaining Taliban resistance are being rooted out in remote tribal regions of the country, Afghanistan's National Army has improved through training exercises with multinational forces. Today 26,600 trained and equipped personnel serve in its ranks, and the Ministry of Interior Police now boasts 57,800 trained officers.

Unlike conventional armies, Islamic terrorists don't fight on a conventional battlefield. They can be anywhere, and often hide out in countries that are America's allies. To counter this challenge, U.S. and Afghan forces are working together to ferret out suspected terrorist safehouses and training sites. At the same time, defense and relief operations must consider the needs of citizens who have suffered under decades of repression.

At the time of the coalition invasion on Afghanistan, only 8% of the population had access to professional health care. The mortality rate for expectant mothers in that country was the highest in the world. Today, thanks to U.S. intervention, at least 80% of the population now has access to basic health care. More than 500 clinics have been set up around the country, serving an average of 340,000 patients each month. Upward of 2,000 indigenous health workers have been trained to provide basic care in rural parts of the country, reaching an estimated 150,000 people per month.

U.S. relief agencies have helped to vaccinate at least 5 million children against basic childhood diseases—an unprecedented first in that country—and physicians have treated more than 700,000 cases of malaria. The United Nations Children's Fund and the World Health Organization, in coordination with U.S. and Afghan forces, have provided vaccinations of 9.9 million children with the polio vaccine.

CONVENTIONAL WISDOM

The war in Afghanistan devastated major cities and towns. The infra-structure and economy are in shambles.

Typical Headlines

"Rough Road Ahead for Afghanistan's Meager Economy"
    —*Washington Post, Dec. 2001*

"Failing Afghanistan"
    —*Boston Globe, Sept. 9, 2006*

"How a 'Good War' in Afghanistan Went Bad"
    —*New York Times, Aug. 12, 2007*

Facts

According to the World Bank, Afghanistan ranks near the top of all nations in the ease of starting a business. More than 3 million land deeds and more than 55,000 businesses have been registered with the government since 2001. Another impressive sign of the energy in the Afghan marketplace is the opening of a new $25 million bottling plant in Kabul by the Coca Cola Company, which employs approximately

500 Afghan workers. U.S. companies such as Ford, 3M, and Boeing are reportedly exploring the possibility of establishing plants there as well.

At the time of the war, Afghan's economy was in the tank. In early 2002, the entire economy was valued at a modest $2.4 billion. By 2006 the economy had more than tripled, to $7.3 billion, and was projected to top $8.8 billion in 2007. At the same time, per capita income has doubled since 2001. The government collected more than $177 million in tax revenues in 2002–2003, and $300 million in 2004–2005. There is now a central bank in Kabul with thirty-two computerized branches. Funds in the Afghanistan central bank are protected by approximately $2 billion in foreign capital reserves.

Regarding basic infrastructure, more than 6,200 miles of road have been built or improved since the collapse of the Taliban regime, with nearly 2,000 miles now in the process of repair. Completion of a new Kabul to Kandahar highway has improved transportation for 30% of the population, and reduced travel times for those two cities from fifteen hours to six hours. Repair and rehabilitation of the Kajaki Dam and surrounding transmission lines has brought electrical power to 1.7 million Afghans in one of the country's most sensitive security areas.

10

Why Gasoline Prices are Rising

CONVENTIONAL WISDOM

Rising oil prices must be related to the war in Iraq. The only reason the U.S. is interested in the Middle East is because of the oil.

Typical Headlines

"Secret U.S. Plans for Iraq's Oil"
    —*BBC, Mar. 17, 2005*

"How Bush's Iraqi Oil Grab Went Awry"
    —*The Nation, Sept. 26, 2007*

"It's About the Oil, Stupid"
    —*Huffington Post, Apr. 14, 2008*

Facts

Global demand for oil in 2008 is expected to top 87 million barrels a day, up 10 million a day from 2001.[1] Iraq's production, which was 2.5 million barrels per day prior to the war, was 2.0 million barrels a

Iraq Oil Production
(million barrels/day)

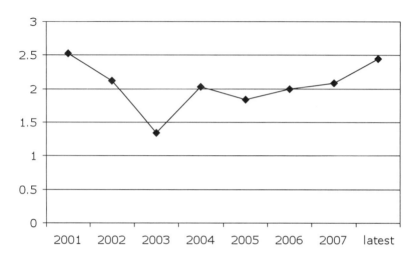

day when the oil shortages began in 2006, and is now back to 2.5 million barrels per day.[2] Clearly Iraq's fluctuation of 0.5 million barrels per day was a very small factor in determining whether or not the global demand surge of 10 million barrels per day could be met. And any change in overall demand or the price of gasoline at the pump has little to do with the amount of oil being produced in Iraq. Additionally, it is likely that without the invasion, Iraq's production would have continued to decline since under the Oil for Food Program, the supply of cash to Iraq's oil industry was insufficient to maintain its infrastructure.

Because oil is a fungible commodity which can be exchanged either for currency or for other goods and commodities of like value, it will make its way to wherever it's needed, regardless whether the producer and consumer governments are friendly to the oil-producing country. If, for example, Iran says, "We will not sell our oil to America; we will sell it to China," Then China will simply buy less oil from Russia, and Russia, in turn, will sell more oil to the U.S.

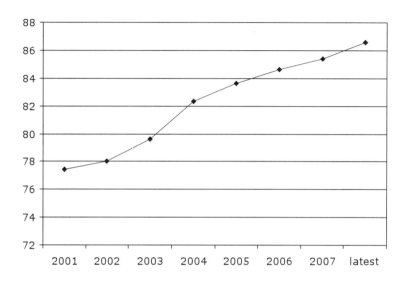

Global Oil Consumption
(million barrels/day)

Much of the increase in global demand is due to growing demand for oil in developing countries, including especially China and India. Since 2005, these two countries have accounted for approximately 70% of the increase in energy demand. And the demand is still increasing. The International Energy Agency (IEA) has predicted that world energy needs will increase 55% by the year 2030. According to an IEA report cited in the *New York Times* in November 2007, net oil imports by China and India are expected to top 19.1 million barrels a day by the year 2030, up from 5.4 million barrels in 2006, and more than the total currently imported by the United States and Japan. By 2030, global oil demand will likely exceed 116 million barrels a day.[3]

The impact of growing demand in these former Third World economies on the price of oil—and the higher costs of consumer goods in both America and Europe—is simply a fact we will have to deal with in the twenty-first century. According to a report in *Time* magazine,

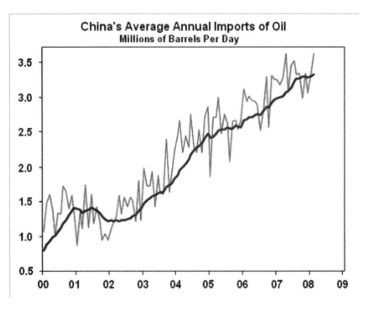

SOURCE: BARCLAYS BANK

China's appetite for oil is a direct result of its booming economy and its newfound appetite for automobiles and other modern conveniences. There's no way that demand can reasonably be seen as the reason for our war in Iraq.[4]

China's oil imports doubled in the first five years of the decade and surged nearly 40% in 2004 alone. These increases made China the leading consumer of oil and energy in the East, and second only to the U.S. as the world's biggest customer for imported oil. And there's no sign that these trends will diminish anytime soon. China's industrial base, says *Time*, is "gobbling up vast amounts of petrochemicals to make everything from fertilizer to Barbie dolls."[5]

Before Complaining Too Loudly

Americans have enjoyed cheap gas and oil for so long we tend to think the recent rise in gas prices is extraordinary and unfair, and in some ways it may be. But before we conclude that we're being punished unfairly, consider what other countries are paying for gasoline at the pump. A 2007 report from the Reuters News Service showed that American fuel prices—fluctuating around $3.50 a gallon in April 2008, according to the Lundberg Survey of fuel prices—are among the lowest on the planet.

Large oil-producing countries like Russia, Mexico, and Saudi Arabia pay lower prices than the U.S., but the vast majority of nations pay a great deal more than the US for oil. Japanese motorists, for example, were paying more than $4.00 for a gallon of gas in 2007; France and Germany were paying $6.50 and higher; Scandinavian drivers were paying in the neighborhood of $7.00 a gallon; and Great Britain topped the list at more than $8.37 per gallon. No one's happy with high fuel prices, but rest assured, it could be a lot worse.[6]

Assessment

Much could have been done to reduce the severity of the current Oil shortage. Irrational opposition to nuclear energy and Congressional blocking of oil drilling in ANWR (Alaska National Wildlife Refuge) and off the shores (but out of sight) of Florida, California and other states can be blamed for the current shortage of domestic oil production. We can agree or disagree with the priorities here, but the fact is these steps could have averted a crisis that had very little to do with Iraq. Nonetheless, seeking energy alternatives is and should be a national priority.

CONVENTIONAL WISDOM

The high price of oil and the outrageous profits made by companies like ExxonMobil and others is because of price-gouging at the expense of the American people.

Typical Headlines

"In Heated Hearings, Oil Bosses Defend Big Profits"
—*MSNBC, Nov. 9, 2005*

"Politicians Call for Oil Price-Gouging Probe"
    —*ABC News, Apr. 24, 2006*

"As Gas Prices Rise Again, Democrats Blame Big Oil"
    —*Washington Post, May 11, 2007*

Facts

In June 2008, intermediate crude oil was selling at a record high price of $135 a barrel on the New York Mercantile Exchange, while the price of gasoline at the pump in many parts of the country was near $4.00 a gallon or higher. There's no question that these high prices have been hard on family budgets, but consumers aren't the only ones complaining. Oil companies have to buy oil at market prices, too; yet, they're expected to keep the price per gallon of gas as low as possible.

The world's cheapest oil to extract from the earth costs approximately $2.00 a barrel and is being pumped at a rate of over 8 million barrels a day in Saudi Arabia. As recently reported by CNN, that oil is generally off-limits to American and European oil companies. Companies like ExxonMobil, Chevron, Shell, and others will spend from $5.00 to $7.00 simply to extract the most easily accessible oil, but that's not all that's involved.[7]

Capital costs to oil producers, such as building and maintenance of pumping facilities and simply keeping qualified workers on the job site, can add an additional $5.00 to $7.00 a barrel in fixed costs, and that's only when the oil is coming from the cheapest regions of the world, such as Azerbaijan. The cost to extract oil from the Gulf of Mexico, Canada, or the Texas coast can boost capital costs another $20 per barrel. On top of that, taxes and royalty payments can range upward of 40% of profits in the United States, and as high as 90% of profits in places like Russia and Libya.

If production were simply a matter of pulling oil out of the ground, big oil companies like ExxonMobil, Chevron, and all the others could make a healthy profit and keep prices at the pump much lower than current prices. But these companies must not only find and extract oil, what they don't find in the ground they must buy. The companies must buy more oil on the commodities market than they produce in order to keep up with high U.S. consumer demand. ExxonMobil, for example, refined 5.6 million barrels a day in the third quarter of 2007, of which only 2.5 million barrels a day were actually produced by ExxonMobil drillers. At the same time, Chevron sold 3.5 million barrels of gasoline and pumped less than half of that.[8]

Assessment

Corporate profits get a lot of media attention these days, but what receives considerably less attention are the taxes paid on corporate profits by the oil producers. The fact is, taxes paid by ExxonMobil exceeded $30 billion in 2007, a record by any standard, and a jump even from the $28 billion in taxes the company paid the previous year. In 2006, Exxon paid $27.9 billion in taxes (a tax rate of 41.4%) on earnings of $67.4 billion; and in 2007 the firm paid $30 billion in taxes on $70.6 billion in total earnings.

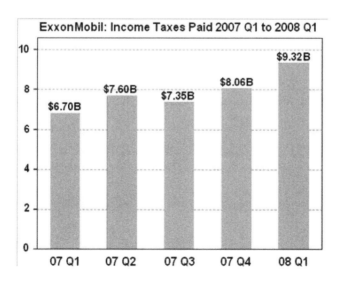

You read that right: Just one big oil company, ExxonMobil, has paid an average of $27 billion annually in taxes over the last three years. To put this in perspective, stock and investment analyst Mark Perry observes that, according to IRS data, 130 million tax returns were filed in this country in 2004 (the most recent year available). The total Adjusted Gross Income for the bottom 50% of taxpayers in that year was $922 billion, and the total income tax paid by that group was $27.4 billion. In other words, as Perry concludes, just one oil company pays as much in taxes to the federal government as the entire bottom 50% of American taxpayers—which, incidentally, is 65,000,000 people.[9]

CONVENTIONAL WISDOM

Oil is yesterday's technology. Biofuels are the future. We have to break our "addiction to oil" and make the move to ethanol and other clean energy solutions.

Typical Headlines

"Ethanol's a Cheaper, Cleaner Alternative"
—*Globe & Mail, Aug. 31, 2004*

"Next Steps on Energy"
—*New York Times, Feb. 6, 2006*

"Researchers Tout Hydrogen Fuel Advance"
—*Boston Globe, Feb. 14, 2004*

Facts

Oil is much more efficient than ethanol and less expensive to produce.

1. It takes more energy to produce a gallon of ethanol than can be generated by a gallon of gas.

2. It takes 1,700 gallons of water to produce one gallon of ethanol.
3. It takes 450 pounds of corn to produce enough ethanol to fill an SUV tank.
4. All ethanol contains water which can damage engine parts.
5. Ethanol is from 20% to 30% less efficient than gasoline, which means you get fewer miles to the gallon with ethanol in your tank.[10]

Even if the total U.S. corn crop were used for ethanol production, it would lower America's dependency on oil no more than 10% to 12%. And because the price of corn has skyrocketed with the ethanol craze, corn farmers in this country are selling to the highest bidder, which means traditional uses of corn for food, cereal, cattle feed, and other products are being neglected. And because of the higher demand for corn, the prices of other grains—such as wheat and soybeans are going up. The impact of ethanol and biofuels production is driving up the price of groceries at your local market.

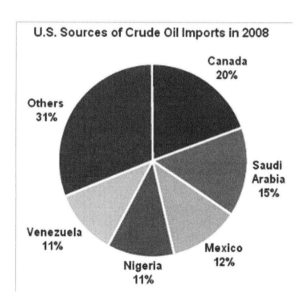

U.S. Sources of Crude Oil Imports in 2008

Canada 20%
Others 31%
Saudi Arabia 15%
Mexico 12%
Nigeria 11%
Venezuela 11%

But, ironically, America is not the only country dealing with the consequences of the biofuels fad. As reported in the *Washington Post*, "Mexico is in the grip of the worst tortilla crisis in its modern history. Dramatically rising international corn prices, spurred by demand for the grain-based fuel ethanol, have led to expensive tortillas." The result is that in some places Mexicans are rioting for lower corn prices.[11] There have also been food riots in Indonesia, Thailand, and China, where rice crops have been confiscated for export and the manufacture of biofuels.

The only way an inefficient, costly, and impractical solution to America's energy needs could survive in a free-market economy is with enormous government subsidies. To encourage farmers to grow corn for ethanol production, Congress paid them a bonus of $9.5 billion in 2005 alone. This is not a practical or efficient system, and every dollar spent by Congress comes out of our pockets, not only in higher taxes, but in higher prices for fuel at the pump. According to the Environmental Working Group, the government spent $41.9 billion on corn subsidies between 1995 and 2004. Yet, because of the popularity of the idea of clean energy and natural biofuels, U.S. investment in ethanol and related technologies, valued at less than $5 billion in 1995, is now projected to top $100 billion by the year 2010.

An editorial in *The Economist* assessed the situation and concluded, "Taxpayers seem not to have noticed they are footing the bill. But corn-based ethanol is neither cheap nor green. It requires almost as much energy to produce (more, say some studies) as it releases when it is burned. And the subsidies on it cost taxpayers, according to the International Institute for Sustainable Development, somewhere between $5.5 billion and $7.3 billion a year."[12]

A six-page cover story on biofuels and clean energy options in the April 7, 2008 issue of *Time* magazine examines the impact of the world's rush to green, including a look, among other things, at the deforestation of the Amazon rainforest of Brazil to plant soybeans and corn crops for biofuels. The article points out that biofuels may be the future, but they're not eco-friendly or clean. Not only do they drive up food prices, but they offer less overall efficiency than petroleum products. Furthermore, the writer concludes, "The world is still going to be fighting an uphill battle until it realizes that right now, biofuels aren't part of the solution at all. They're part of the problem."[13]

CONVENTIONAL WISDOM

The oil companies are making unfair profits because of high gas prices. It's time for Congress to enact a Windfall Profits Tax, like they did back in the 1980s.

Typical Headlines

"Tax the Windfall"
—*Washington Post, Apr. 28, 2006*

"Gas Industry Accused of Price Gouging"
—*ABC News, Feb. 21, 2003*

"Soaring Earnings Prompt Calls For a Windfall Profit Tax"
—*CNN Money, Oct. 28, 2005*

Facts

The windfall profits tax is a tax levied on oil producers when the price of oil exceeds a certain level. Over the past five years, Democrats in Congress have repeatedly tried to pass laws imposing an additional 50% tax on the price of oil when the price goes above $40 per barrel. At the April 2008 market price of about $120 per barrel, each barrel sold or refined would be taxed an additional 50% on the so-called $80 "windfall" above $40, or another $40. This tax would be imposed on top of the 35% to 40% federal income tax and other regulatory fees already being paid by the industry. Under those rules why would any company take the risks of trying to find new oil fields?

Public dissatisfaction with the high price of gas may incline some people to believe that it's only fair to stick it to the "big oil" companies by raising their taxes, particularly when some in Congress have said that those taxes could be rebated to the taxpayers. The fact is, higher taxes on gasoline will always come back as higher priced fuels, as well as higher taxes for consumers. At a time when the oil industry is searching for better options and more accessible sources of crude oil, a "windfall profits tax" is the wrong idea at the wrong time.

The last time such a tax was tried in the 1980s, it backfired badly. The new higher taxes discouraged the oil industry from expanding operations or finding new domestic energy supplies, and ultimately led to a surge of oil imports from the Middle East and elsewhere, which led, in turn, to further escalation of prices at the pump. According to a 1990 study by the Congressional Research Service, the windfall profits tax in place from 1980 to 1988 "reduced domestic oil production from between 3% and 6%, and increased oil imports from between 8 and 16%."[14] In the end, the tax hurt consumers more than it helped, and the projected tax revenues turned out to be much lower than originally predicted because of the negative impact on production.[15]

Assessment

A basic law of Economics 101 is that whatever you tax you get less of, and whatever you subsidize you get more of. Another basic principle is that when supply exceeds demand, prices go down, and when demand exceeds the supply, prices go up. The more government penalizes new business development by over-taxing profits, the more it reduces the incentive for corporations in the high-risk energy business to find, refine, and produce more fuel. As in the 1980s, such taxes will have precisely the opposite effect of what has been promised by overzealous lawmakers.

When President Carter signed the "Crude Oil Windfall Profits Tax" into law in April 1980, it was the largest tax ever imposed on an

American industry. The money was supposed to be used to develop renewable energy, but the tax failed to deliver. Domestic production dropped by 6% while imports increased from 8% to 16%, until the tax was finally repealed by President Reagan in 1988. According to the Congressional Research Service, Carter's tax raised a total of $40 billion, instead of the $227 billion that had been projected, and generated no revenue at all after 1986, because oil prices fell and production dropped.[16]

A free-market economy rewards responsible risk-taking, and America's big oil companies are engaged in a high-risk business. Maintaining production facilities, refineries, and pipelines involves enormous costs under adverse conditions, including the demands of exploration, the harsh physical and weather conditions encountered by oil-field workers, and the high levels of security required in many places to ensure that oil pumped from the earth actually makes it to its final destination.

Profits from all this effort come only years after the investments are made, and political instability and changing global markets can turn everything upside down in a heartbeat. When members of Congress—or our so-called "consumer advocates"—insist on taking the rewards out of the risks and destroying the private oil companies' incentive to invest, nobody wins except OPEC that would end up controlling a greater percentage of the available supply.

11

A Scandal Not to Be Ignored

CONVENTIONAL WISDOM

The United Nations Oil-for-Food scandal was really no big deal. The media just used it to try and embarrass the United Nations.

Typical Headlines:

"The Wrong Way to Reform the U.N."
 —*Seattle Post-Intelligencer, June 17, 2005*

"Annan: U.N. Embarrassed by Report—Rejects Call to Resign after Probe into Oil-For-Food Failures"
 —*CBS News, Sept. 7, 2005*

Facts

In terms of the amounts of money involved, the scale of corruption, and the disservice to the beleaguered people of Iraq, the Oil-for-Food scandal was enormous. Many officials confessed to and/or were convicted of crimes.

The United Nations Oil-for-Food Program began with the best of intentions. Under the U.N. sanctions of the early 1990's, the international community had agreed not to purchase Oil from Iraq until the government complied with the requirements of U.N. security council resolutions. The lack of oil revenue caused severe hardship for the people of Iraq, and the Oil-for-Food Program was designed to allow the government of Iraq to sell a certain portion of its oil under U.N. supervision to finance purchases of medical supplies and other humanitarian aids. The process was designed to provide revenue from oil, but prevent the Iraqi regime from using it to reconstitute its army and replenish Saddam's supplies of weapons of mass destruction.

The sanctions could have been lifted at any time if Saddam had simply chosen to comply with U.N. Security Council resolutions. But he chose, instead, to show his contempt by ignoring the resolutions and manipulating the Oil-for-Food program to his own advantage. The program was established by the U.N. Security Council in April 1995. According to the official U.N. website, $65 billion in revenues from Iraqi oil was dispersed for humanitarian purposes. Of the total, 72% was used for humanitarian aid, and the balance was used to pay reparations in Kuwait and surrounding countries. Approximately 3% was spent on operational costs by the U.N. and its inspection teams in Iraq. At least, that's what the official records stated.[1]

After the fall of Baghdad in 2003, papers surfaced in the files of the former government and its oil ministry indicating that the head of the U.N. Oil-for-Food program, Mr. Benon Sevan, may have taken as much as $1.2 million in bribes and illegal transfers for himself. After a period of denials and counter-claims, the U.N. eventually set up an internal commission to investigate the program, and selected former Federal Reserve Chairman Paul Volcker to lead the effort.

The Commission Report
The Volcker Commission report, released on Oct. 27, 2005, revealed the following:

- Of 248 companies that purchased oil, 139 paid illicit "surcharges" which made their way to the Iraqi government. Many of these companies may not have known the payments were illicit. Of the 3,614 companies that sold humanitarian goods to Iraq, 2,253 paid "kickbacks." Again, some may not have understood fully what was going on.

- Illicit payments enriched Saddam and his government by $1.8 billion.

- Companies in France and Russia were explicitly chosen for allocations to reward their attempts to influence the global political process in favor of Saddam's government.

- Illicit payments were made to officials for their influence. Those officials were disproportionately French, but also included people in the U.S. and U.K. who were publicly opposed to the U.N. sanctions, such as the British MP George Galloway.

- Benon Sevan, the U.N. program leader, was found to have solicited kickbacks from the Iraqi government. While Sevan may have pocketed more than a million dollars, records revealed $160,000 of personal income for which he offered several contradictory explanations, He first claimed the money was from an elderly aunt in Cyprus, who died from a fall down an elevator shaft. During the investigation, Sevan took a lengthy vacation and then retirement, back to his native Cyprus. He remains under a U.S. federal indictment, but, according to the laws of Cyprus, cannot be extradited to stand trial.

- It was discovered that Alexander Yakovlev, the U.N. procurement officer tasked with choosing suppliers to coordinate shipments of humanitarian goods, ended up receiving more than $1 million in illicit funds and kickbacks from U.N. contractors outside the Oil-for-Food program. He pleaded guilty in a U.S. court to money laundering and illegal wire transfers and, after three years of court deliberations, is awaiting sentencing on convictions that could put him away for up to twenty years.

Follow the Money

The Volcker Report said that the government of Iraq especially favored individuals and companies based in France in its distribution of oil allocations. Records seized in Iraq showed that French companies contracted for $4.4 billion of oil from Iraq, second only to Russian companies, in spite of the fact that, unlike Russia, France has almost no oil industry to speak of. Iraq's preference for French companies even led some firms in other countries to disguise themselves as being French-based. Vitol S.A., a Switzerland-based company, purchased Iraq oil under the name "Vitol France" even though no such company had ever existed.

Documents reviewed by the House of Representatives committee chaired by Republican Norm Coleman showed that Saddam Hussein may have received more than $21 billion in illicit oil revenues from smuggling and illicit Oil-for-Food payments, which he used to buy friends and favors around the world.

The Volker Commission report found that the following people of influence had received illicit compensation in the form of oil vouchers from Saddam Hussein:

Jean-Bernard Mérimée. In 2005, one of France's most distinguished diplomats, Jean-Bernard Mérimée, confessed to accepting oil allocations for 11 million barrels of oil from Saddam in 2002. In addition, $165,700 was deposited in offshore accounts in his name in Morocco. Mérimée, who holds the title "ambassador for life," carried out his illicit activity while serving as Special Advisor to the Secretary General of the United Nations, with the rank of Under-Secretary-General. He also served as president of the United Nations Security Council intermittently from 1991 to 1995 while he was France's permanent representative to the U.N.

Georges Pasqua and Bernard Guillet. Georges Pasqua, a former interior minister and a close political ally of former President Jacques Chirac for the past 30 years, received allocations of 11 million barrels of oil during 1999 and 2000. Tables of Iraq's Oil Company (SOMO) labeled these allocations simply "France." The transactions were executed by Bernard Guillet on behalf of Mr. Pasqua. After denying that any such transactions occurred, bank records revealed deposits and withdrawals of $234,000 through a Swiss bank account to Mr. Guillet. Mr. Guillet was arrested in Paris in April 2005, in connection with the Oil-for-Food inquiry. He was released on bail and was subsequently elected to the French Senate, where he enjoys immunity from criminal prosecution.

Claude Kaspereit, an associate of **Marc Rich & Co.** Claude Kaspereit, son of the French Member of Parliament Gabriel Kaspereit, was allocated over 9.5 million barrels of oil from Iraq. He used a France-based shell company. Marc Rich & Co. financed the deal and demanded that the identity of the company be kept secret. In June, 2000, Kaspereit chartered a flight to Iraq without U.N. authorization and in violation of the international embargo, solely to generate publicity against the sanctions. This act of defiance was welcomed by Saddam Hussein and was quickly rewarded with the enormous oil allocation.

Serge Boidevaix, former Director of the French Department for North Africa and the Middle East—serving as the head of France's diplomatic service in the region and an officer of the French Ministry of Foreign Affairs—received more than 32 million barrels, as detailed in the Volcker Report. **Gilles Munier,** Secretary-General of the French-Iraqi Friendship Association, received a voucher allocation of 11.8 million barrels.

Other noteworthy individuals implicated in the scandal include British Member of Parliament **George Galloway**, who was allocated "a total of over 18 million barrels of oil," either directly, "or in the name of one of his associates, **Fawaz Abdullah Zureikat**." According to official records, "Mr. Zureikat received commissions for handling the sale of approximately 11 million barrels that were allocated in Mr. Galloway's name." These oil allocations were specifically granted to fund Mr. Galloway's anti-sanctions activities. Iraqi officials identified Mr. Zureikat as acting on Mr. Galloway's behalf to conduct oil transactions in Baghdad.

Roberto Formigioni, President of the Lombardy Region of Italy, was granted a total of over 27 million barrels of oil by the government of Iraq. Over 24.1 million barrels of this oil were lifted. Several Russian political parties and politicians received allocations of Iraqi oil as well, including the Communist Party of the Russian Federation (125.1 million barrels); **Vladimir Zhirinovsky** and the Liberal Democratic Party of Russia (73 million barrels); the Party of Peace and Unity (55.5 million barrels); and **Alexander Voloshin**, Chief of Staff to Russian President **Vladimir Putin** (4.3 million barrels).

Several Americans were also implicated, tried, and sentenced in connection with the scandal, including Texas oilman **David Chalmers** and three associates, whose Bayoil Inc. refinery business had paid up to $1 million in illegal surcharges to the Iraqi government for the rights to purchase oil outside the limits of international sanctions. A complete listing of the individuals, companies, and governments found in Iraqi records to be complicit in receiving illicit oil vouchers can be found in a January 2004 article in the British newspaper, *The Independent*. The list of vouchers totals 4.2 trillion barrels of oil.[2]

It is also worth noting that Jacques Chirac also had a longstanding relationship with Saddam Hussein dating back to 1974 when he, then French Premier, traveled to Iraq to meet Hussein, then Iraq's Vice President, to discuss the sale of nuclear reactors. In 1975 Chirac personally gave Hussein a tour of parts of France and a nuclear plant. Later, Chirac would say publicly that had a "close personal relationship with Saddam Hussein."[3]

Assessment

It is not difficult to imagine the thoughts of the high ranking French officials listed above in late 2002 as the invasion was being debated around the world. If Iraq is invaded, incriminating documents will be revealed, names and careers destroyed, and jail might follow. If Iraq is *not* invaded, kickbacks and the purchase of new vacation homes continues. How would you imagine they advised their friend Mr. Chirac?

Given the close relationship Mr. Chirac had with Saddam Hussein, and the significant value that relationship meant to France, it is not difficult to see why France would have decided, after voting for "serious consequences," to then change and promise to veto those consequences when it came time to implement them.

The U.S. ended up being widely blamed for taking up a just and difficult cause in Iraq, while France and Russia were portrayed as having been wise for resisting it even though it was probably corruption within their countries that tipped the scale against rather than in favor of supporting the effort. This unfair contrast fit the narrative of many around the world.

CONVENTIONAL WISDOM

The U.S. went out of its way to make the French government look bad. The only reason was to deflect attention from our own mistakes.

Typical Headlines

"France Says It Is Victim of Smear Campaign"
    —*CNN, May 19, 2003*

"France Warns Iraq War Would Divide World"
    —*USA Today, Feb. 26, 2003*

Facts

At every stage of Saddam's deceptions, French and Russian companies were in it up to their eyeballs. For years the French sold high performance Dassault Mirage fighter aircraft to the Iraqi Air Force, and French engineers helped build and install power stations and nuclear research labs, including the Osiraq nuclear reactor destroyed by Israel bombers in 1981.

No fewer than 46 Russian and 11 French names appear on the Iraqi Oil Ministry's list of individuals and governments receiving oil vouchers from Saddam. The Russian government is alleged to have received $1.36 billion in oil vouchers. Prior to the U.S. invasion and regime change in April 2003, French and Russian oil companies held oil contracts with the Iraqi government amounting to 40% of the entire oil wealth of the country.

> When the Iraqi regime learned of attempts by companies to dis-guise themselves as French entities, Iraqi officials explicitly referred to France as a favored trading partner. There is no doubt that the U.N. relief effort in Iraq has been a global scandal. A monstrous dictator was able to turn the Oil-for-Food program into a cash cow for himself and his inner circle, leaving Iraqis further deprived as he bought influence abroad and acquired the arms and munitions that coalition forces discovered when they invaded Iraq. . . . But Saddam's ability to reap billions for himself, his cronies, and those who proved useful to him abroad depended on individuals who were his counterparties.[4]

Assessment

Saddam was within his right to favor French companies over American and British firms. Furthermore, it was his right to reward those who agreed with his policies. However, it seems highly likely that the out-spoken resistance of countries like France and Russia to Resolution 1441, and the decision to remove Saddam from power, had more to do with protecting their own financial interests in that country than with any concern for doing what was right. And neither of those countries was within their rights in accepting massive kickbacks and payoffs while blocking the coalition's efforts at every turn.

12

Progress on Nuclear Challenges

CONVENTIONAL WISDOM

America's arrogance and "go it alone" diplomacy has only made worsened nuclear risks.

Typical Quotes

"It is important for us to rebuild a nuclear non-proliferation strategy—something that this administration, frankly, has ignored, and has made us less safe as a consequence."
> —*Barack Obama, during Democratic debates at St. Anselm College in New Hampshire, Jan. 5, 2008*

"Recent improvements to the U.S. arsenal aimed at achieving nuclear dominance are stimulating Russia to increase its spending on nuclear weapons. As a result, both sides are raising the likelihood of nuclear war, whether intentional or accidental."
> —*Christian Science Monitor, Apr. 26, 2006.*

"The Administration's fitful attempts at nuclear diplomacy have
been undermined by its proud contempt for multilateral-treaty
regimes . . . when President Bush came to office, he showed
little interest in the non-proliferation regime or its goals."
    —Steve Coll, *The New Yorker*, Oct. 23, 2006

Facts

The Nuclear Non Proliferation Treaty (NPT) was written in 1968,
shortly after France and China became the fourth and fifth nations to
develop nuclear capabilities. The world was in a nuclear arms race,
and United Nations leaders agreed:

> Considering the devastation that would be visited upon all
> mankind by a nuclear war and the consequent need to make
> every effort to avert the danger of such a war and to take meas-
> ures to safeguard the security of peoples . . .
>   Believing that the proliferation of nuclear weapons would
> seriously enhance the danger of nuclear war . . .

The writers believed the spread of nuclear technology would expo-
nentially increase the likelihood that nuclear weapons would eventually find their way into the hands of men who would use them for
unthinkable purposes. By signing the treaty, more than 150 countries
gave up their right to nuclear weapons in the interest of the greater
good, "the easing of international tension and the strengthening of trust
between States," and the hope of someday creating the conditions for
a halt to the production of these instruments of potential horror.

The world leaders who advanced this treaty had fought and lived
through World War II. They knew the evil that men can do. Hitler,
Mussolini, Hirohito, and Stalin were as much a part of their lives as
the Bushes and Clintons are a part of our own. They were not naïve;
they understood that if powerful weapons were available, they would
likely be used. The 1962 Cuban Missile Crisis kept the risks of a

nuclear nightmare fresh in their minds. They understood the destruction that could occur at any time, and that if weapons moved into the hands of those who had nothing to lose, the loss to mankind could be of unimaginable proportions.

But let's be quick to say that nuclear power is not the problem. Peaceful uses of nuclear energy will no doubt become more important as technology and populations expand in the twenty-first century. The problem is that some maniac with a hot temper and a nuclear trigger could level an American city just to prove his manhood. So far there's no evidence suggesting that the belligerent Iranian President Mahmoud Ahmadinejad or the North Korea's Kim Jong-il are any more rational than Adolf Hitler or Hirohito. We know for certain that al-Qaeda and other Islamic extremists would love nothing better than to annihilate America.

What the Treaty Actually Says

Article I: Each nuclear-weapon State Party to the Treaty undertakes not to transfer to any recipient whatsoever nuclear weapons or other nuclear explosive devices or control over such weapons or explosive devices directly, or indirectly; and not in any way to assist, encourage, or induce any non-nuclear-weapon State to manufacture or otherwise acquire nuclear weapons or other nuclear explosive devices, or control over such weapons or explosive devices.

Article II: Each non-nuclear-weapon State Party to the Treaty undertakes not to receive the transfer from any transferor whatsoever of nuclear weapons or other nuclear explosive devices or of control over such weapons or explosive devices directly, or indirectly; not to manufacture or otherwise acquire nuclear weapons or other nuclear explosive devices; and not to seek or receive any assistance in the manufacture of nuclear weapons or other nuclear explosive devices.[1]

Further, the NPT requires non-nuclear-weapon countries to accept
safeguard measures, including unannounced inspections by qualified
U.N. personnel, to verify compliance with the terms of the treaty. It is
this portion of the NPT that has created the controversy with countries like Iraq, Iran, and North Korea.

Only four countries have not signed the NPT: India, Israel, Pakistan, and North Korea. This means that nations like Iran and Iraq have
signed and ratified the treaty, even though we now know their commitment was not honored. India and Pakistan both possess and have tested
nuclear weapons. Israel, however, has had a policy of "opacity" regarding its own nuclear weapons program, meaning that they have given
hints that they have them but have never publicly acknowledged the fact.

Importantly, of the five nations that posed a nuclear threat during
George Bush's presidency, three have been eliminated (Iraq, Libya, and
Syria), and another (North Korea) appears to be on the verge of being
eliminated.[2] The Bush approach to nuclear countries was the opposite
of "go it alone." In fact, he was criticized during the 2004 election for
not agreeing to unilateral (i.e., "go it alone") talks with North Korea.
Here are the facts related to these various nuclear programs.

North Korea: For more than a decade, the United States and
North Korea's neighbors tried various approaches to prevent North
Korea from becoming nuclear. The Bush administration argued that a
multilateral approach had a better chance, because North Korea
would use one-on-one negotiations as a chance to divide our allies—
China, Japan, South Korea, and Russia. Early on, North Korea ratified
the NPT, then promptly violated it and later withdrew. Eventually,
however, on February 13, 2007 they signed an agreement with all six
nations to shut down their nuclear program in exchange for $250 mil-
lion worth of oil. By this point, they needed money more than they
needed the weapons. If it is successful, a stalemate lasting almost
twenty years will have been broken.

Libya: After the invasion of Iraq and the fall of Baghdad in 2003,
Libyan leader Muammar Qaddafi apparently saw the handwriting on

the wall and volunteered to end his nuclear development activities and turn over all technology and equipment to the International Atomic Energy Agency (IAEA). Officials overseeing the dismantling of Libya's weapons program reported that it was "much further advanced" than U.S. and British intelligence agencies once believed, and included centrifuges and a uranium-enrichment program, all necessary components in making a nuclear bomb.

Syria: We may not know all the places where nuclear weapons are hidden. After Libya gave up its development program, details were discovered about the network established by the renegade Pakistani nuclear engineer, A. Q. Khan, to sell nuclear secrets to Third World tyrants. But the one thing that became perfectly clear was that the science of nuclear technology was out there, and it was for sale. The nation of Syria is a case in point. It appeared to military analysts that Syria's Al Kibar facility was indeed a copy of North Korea's Yongbyon complex, as "the grid of cylinders for control rods and refueling ports" were "arrayed almost identically."[3] With the risks to the entire Middle East posed by nuclear weapons in the hands of a Syrian dictator, it's not surprising that Israel felt their right of peaceful coexistence, and their survival as a nation, demanded the destruction of that facility.[4]

Assessment

It is completely unreported that much progress has been made in recent years on nuclear proliferation, one of the most important issues of our time. Of the five nations that posed a potential nuclear threat when President Bush took office, three (Iraq, Libya, and Syria) have been eliminated and another (North Korea) appears to be on the verge of elimination. This is a as a result, not of "go it alone diplomacy," but of multilateral pressure and strength.

Nuclear proliferation has been one of the thorniest issues confronting U.S. presidents ever since President Harry Truman ordered the strike that ended World War II. The nuclear non-proliferation treaty has worked because successful nations have a common desire to see proliferation stopped. The current success demonstrates the power of the U.S. when it works closely with the Europeans, China, Russia and Japan to a common purpose.

CONVENTIONAL WISDOM

Iran's nuclear program is only for peaceful purposes now. After all, the National Intelligence Estimate (NIE) said that Iran had stopped developing nuclear weapons in 2003.

Typical Headlines

"U.S. Intel: Iran Stopped Nuke Program in 2003"
—*U.S. News & World Report, Dec. 4, 2007*

"A Blow to Bush's Tehran Policy"
—*Washington Post, Dec. 4, 2007*

Facts

Thomas Fingar, the chairman of the National Intelligence Council which produced the NIE Report, told analysts at the Council on Foreign Relations that he stands by the NIE's conclusions. But he quickly added that his office never thought those conclusions would ever become public. "If we thought for a minute they would be released, which we didn't, we would have framed them somewhat differently." Asked how he would have framed them, he said:

Dear Readers . . .

You can't have a bomb unless you have fissile material . . . the Iranians continue to develop fissile material. A weapon is not much good if you can't deliver it—they have a missile-development program. But you don't have a bomb unless you can produce a device and weaponize it. That's what's stopped.[5]

Or as *The Economist's* blogger assessed the NIE Chairman's remarks: "Be afraid, but not too afraid." Ronald Reagan's oft-quoted phrase, "Trust, but verify," would seem to apply as well.

Assessment

More recent analysis suggests that the NIE Report's claims that Iran was out of the nuke business were actually wrong, or at least misleading. CIA Director Michael Hayden said recently that it was "hard for me to explain" the conclusions reached in the 2003 National Intelligence Estimate on Iran's nuclear weapons program. So now the conclusion that Iran had stopped work on its weapons program is being downplayed by the same officials who wrote the report.

In his unscripted response to questions from a member of the audience at the National Press Club, Hayden said, "Why would the Iranians be willing to pay the international tariff they appear to be willing to pay for what they're doing now if they did not have, at a minimum . . . at a minimum . . . if they did not have a desire to keep the option open to develop a nuclear weapon and, perhaps even more so, that they have already decided to do that?"

The Survey Says

A Rasmussen survey found that 67% of American voters believe that Iran remains a threat to the security of the United States. Only 19% disagree while 14% are not sure. Fifty-nine percent (59%) believe that the United States should continue sanctions against Iran. Twenty percent (20%) disagree and 21% are not sure.

Meanwhile, 47% believe it is "Very Likely" that Iran will develop nuclear weapons in the future and another 34% believe Iran is "Somewhat Likely" to do so. Twenty-nine percent (29%) of liberal voters believe Iran has stopped its weapons program but 54% disagree. Among conservatives, just 8% believe Iran has stopped, while 81% disagree.[6]

Most of the news coverage of the NIE Report focused on the first sentence, which said: "We judge with high confidence that in fall 2003, Tehran halted its nuclear weapons program." But officials now say the sentence refers only to work on a nuclear warhead. Director of National Intelligence Michael McConnell said the report was so quickly declassified and poorly focused that it confused people.

"If I had it to do over again," he told a Senate panel, "I would be very specific in how I described what was canceled and what continued." Intelligence experts are now emphasizing that Iran is still working on its enrichment program, which could be used to make weapons and ballistic missiles, which could be used to deliver a nuclear warhead, which could strike Europe and, potentially, the United States. Which means, he thinks we need keep an eye on Iran.[7]

CONVENTIONAL WISDOM

Why does the United States get to dictate whether or not North Korea or Iran has nuclear weapons, anyway? They're free countries. Isn't that really their decision?

Typical Headlines

"Why Shouldn't Iran Have Nuclear Weapons?
   Israel has American Warheads Ready to Fire"
      —*The Independent, Apr. 30, 2006*

"Nuclear Hypocrisy: To avoid War, Bush Should Engage in Direct Negotiations with Iran"
      —*Joe Conason, Salon.com, Oct. 19, 2007*

Facts

First of all, neither Syria, nor North Korea, nor Iran could conceivably meet anyone's definition of a "free country"—far from it. The citizens of these countries are virtual prisoners of the state, and suffer under repressive leadership. Secondly, none of the leaders of these countries can be trusted to tell the truth. Under the Framework Agreement negotiated by the Clinton administration, North Korea had agreed to place its store of uranium fuel rods in a secure facility guarded by international weapons-inspectors. In October 2002, North Korean negotiators from Pyongyang began demanding one-on-one talks with Washington. The U.S., however, insisted on multilateral talks involving at least one other nation, such as China, since North Korea's desire to join the nuclear club was primarily a regional problem.

After the U.S. victory in Iraq, the North Koreans reluctantly agreed that China should participate in multilateral discussions. But it wasn't long until Kim Jung Il abruptly expelled the U.N. weapons inspectors, broke the seals on the locks, and had the fuel rods removed to underground laboratories where North Korean engineers began the process of converting them into weapons-grade plutonium.

In a lengthy report on the war of words between Washington and Pyongyang, *Newsweek* reporters offered the following assessment:

> No one in Washington has ever known quite how to deal with North Korea. As a lonely Stalinist regime, Kim's nation is a political toxic-waste site that has festered for 50 years amid East Asia's glittering successes. It is also a place of truly Orwellian oddity, where traffic cops in Pyongyang's empty boulevards go through the motions of directing cars when there are none, where thousands of people starve unnoticed and where Kim administers "a gulag the size of Houston," in Bush's words. Bill Clinton likewise despised Kim, and as president, Clinton came much closer than Bush ever has to attacking him.[8]

North Korea is certainly a special case, but the disputes and saber-rattling taking place in that part of the world illustrate why an ongoing program of nuclear deterrence is so important. Ignoring the threats and belligerence of Iran regarding its nuclear ambitions could prove to be an even costlier mistake. Mahmoud Ahmadinejad has threatened to wipe Israel off the map, denies that the Holocaust ever happened, despises the United States and the West, and supports terrorism and other types of radicalism around the world. Any mention by his own country's citizens of free democratic elections, freedom of speech, or freedom of the press is an open invitation to violent suppression by the totalitarian state's riot police.

As one foreign policy insider has observed, "Unlike the Soviet Union, which was at least predictable enough to deter, Iran is simply too radical, unstable, and contemptuous of both international law and basic standards of decency to be allowed into the nuclear club. The world has already seen human rights-abusing regimes with nuclear weapons in the former Soviet Union and China. It does not need another."[9]

Assessment

The dangers of a nuclear world in which Stalinist tyrants like those in North Korea and Theocrats in Iran can bargain and blackmail the international community into accepting their dictates is not a place where any of us would want to live. The only way to make sure that such a scenario never happens is for those nations that are dedicated to peaceful coexistence to use whatever political, diplomatic, or military muscle they possess to demand compliance with the goals of nuclear non-proliferation. From day one, the United States has offered the strongest and most clear-headed vision of how this can be accomplished.

A survey in a study published in the 2002 winter edition of the journal *International Security* reveals that there have been twenty cases of "nuclear reversal"—in which a country currently pursuing nuclear weapons halts or rolls back its nuclear program—over the lifetime of the Nuclear Non-Proliferation Treaty. The article also noted that the U.S. has played a "critical role . . . in arresting nuclear proliferation," and concluded that "sustained U.S. encouragement of perceptions [that acquiring nuclear technology has limited utility] . . . and a conscious U.S.-led effort to complicate the road to nuclear weapons" are the two most important reasons for the success of these reversals.

WARHEADS

COUNTRY	WARHEADS ACTIVE/TOTAL*	YEAR OF FIRST TEST
Five nuclear weapons states from the NPT		
United States	5,163 / 9,938	1945 ("Trinity")
Russia	5,830 / 16,000	1949 ("RDS-1")
United Kingdom	<200	1952 ("Hurricane")
France	350	1960 ("Gerboise Bleue")
China	200	1964 ("596")
Other known nuclear powers		
India	70–120	1974 ("Smiling Buddha")
Pakistan	30–80	1998 ("Chagai-I")
North Korea	1–10	2006 (The Beginning)[12]
Undeclared nuclear weapons states		
Israel	75–200	Unknown / or 1979

An Explosive Situation

The writer of the journal article then goes on to say that:

> The United States has been continuously engaged in inno-
> vative, interdepartmental, and multilateral non-proliferation
> efforts since 9/11. In fact, far from ignoring non-proliferation
> issues, this administration has actually devoted more resources
> to counter-proliferation since it came into office, doubling
> DOE's nuclear non-proliferation budget from fiscal year 2001
> to fiscal year 2006 and spearheaded two significant, underre-
> ported multilateral initiatives on combating global nuclear
> terror—U.N. Security Council Resolution 1540 and the Pro-
> liferation Security Initiative—and have continually reaffirmed
> its' commitment to fulfill its disarmament obligations under
> the SORT, the 2001 successor to the SALT, START I and
> START II treaties it signed with Russia during the cold war.[10]

It has been estimated that there are currently in the neighborhood of 20,000 nuclear weapons in the world. At one time there were as many as 65,000 nuclear weapons, but thanks to the NPT accords and America's record of vigilance, that number has been voluntarily reduced. Writing in the *Washington Post*, columnist Robert Samuelson writes that, "It must be counted as a major miracle of the modern age that in the 59 years since Hiroshima and Nagasaki none of them has been used in anger."[11] And we say, let's keep it that way.

III

Domestic Issues

13

Rethinking Katrina

CONVENTIONAL WISDOM

Most of the suffering in the aftermath of Hurricane Katrina resulted from the arrogance and incompetence of FEMA and the Bush Administration.

Typical Headlines

"FEMA Was Unprepared for Katrina Relief Effort, Insiders Say"
—*ABC News, Sept. 8, 2005*

"FEMA, Slow to the Rescue, Now Stumbles in Aid Effort"
—*New York Times, Sept. 17, 2005*

"'Abolish' FEMA, Says Bipartisan Senate Panel"
—*USA Today, Apr. 27, 2006*

Facts

Hurricane Katrina was a horrific disaster for the city of New Orleans and the U.S. Gulf Coast. Lengthy accounts of all that happened during those dreadful days and weeks, both good and bad, have been reported in meticulous detail, not only in the major media, but in several books published in 2006 and 2007. Here's a summary of the major events:

Katrina strengthened in the Gulf of Mexico to an ominous Category 5 hurricane with sustained winds of 175 miles per hour and gusts up to 200 miles per hour before making landfall as a Category 3 storm on the morning of August 29, 2005. In coming days, more than 1,300 people would lose their lives as a result of the storm.

The first levees were breached by the pounding surf on Sunday. Then, on Monday morning, Katrina made landfall. By Wednesday, 80% of the city was under water. Everything not nailed down was swept away. According to one report from the National Association of Counties, St. Bernard Parish had a pre-storm population of 65,554. A year later, no more than 6,000 people were still living there.

"When Katrina first came ashore, it came ashore in Plaquemines," said the Parish President. "What the wind didn't get, the water did."[1] The small town of Empire was literally erased from the map. Roughly 60% of the 29,969 residents of the parish were finally able to return home by mid-2007. Both St. Bernard and Plaquemines Counties, which are part of the Greater New Orleans metropolitan area, where shattered by the hurricane.

The infrastructure of New Orleans and more than a dozen surrounding communities was utterly devastated. Stores, shops, and office buildings were swamped, and more than 142,000 homes and apartments were destroyed. As late as February 20, 2006, six months after the initial devastation, electricity was still being restored to the narrow peninsula where most of Louisiana's oil and gas industry was located.

As tragic as that hurricane was, the most serious catastrophe wasn't the storm itself. Of course the winds, rain, and flooding that pounded a major American city were disastrous, but Katrina was a bad hurricane like others FEMA had handled with remarkable success over the previous three years. But the levees were the real problem, and that's a story with a long and sad history.

When the levees broke, the potential for a full-scale humanitarian disaster was increased by many fold. The American Red Cross, which received its share of criticism by the media after the event, said that Katrina was the biggest relief effort they had ever encountered, by a factor of 20. After the storm, FEMA and Bush administration officials were severely criticized for not responding quickly enough, and many people came to believe that the rescue effort was a major fiasco. If you happen to be one of them, here are some facts you may not be aware of:

- By Monday, August 29th, the day Katrina made landfall, 65 National Guard helicopters were positioned throughout the Gulf Coast region. Pilots were on 24-hour alert.
- Helicopter rescue missions began 4 hours after landfall, even before the winds subsided. Coast Guard teams alone rescued over 33,000 people, six times the annual average for the Coast Guard nationally.
- Local organizations, such as Wildlife and Fisheries officers, rescued another 10,000 people with a force of 200 rescuers using boats and safety gear.
- 6,000 National Guard troops were called up from the affected states by Monday morning. 8,000 were on call by Tuesday. By Thursday, nearly 22,000 National Guard soldiers and airmen had been deployed to the region, including 6,500 in New Orleans alone, setting an all-time record for the largest ever response to a domestic emergency.[2]
- 25 of FEMA's 28 national Urban and Rescue Incident Support Teams were deployed to the Gulf Coast to support the Katrina relief effort.[3]

At about noon on Tuesday, it became apparent that the levees could not be saved—even with massive 3,000-pound sandbags being dropped by helicopters. It was then that Katrina became much more than a bad hurricane. Three others had already hit either Florida or Louisiana that year without this level of devastation. That afternoon Louisiana governor Kathleen Blanco decided to evacuate the Superdome. Within one hour of the decision, FEMA tasked the U.S. Dept of Transportation with assembling a fleet of over 1,100 vehicles—while the city's perfectly fine buses sat unused as the water rose. Significant numbers of federally con- tracted buses began arriving at the Superdome on Wednesday afternoon, and carried thousands of evacuees to the Houston Astrodome. By Friday morning, approximately 15,000 people had been evacuated from the Superdome, leaving approximately 5,500. The evacuation was finished before dawn Saturday morning, September 3.

What is FEMA?

According to their own literature, the mission of the Federal Emergency Management Agency is to reduce loss of life and property and protect the nation from all major hazards—including natural disasters, acts of terrorism, and other man-made disasters—by leading and supporting the nation in a risk-based, comprehensive emergency management sys- tem of preparedness, protection, response, recovery, and mitigation.

The agency is staffed by 2,600 full-time employees in Washington D.C. and at area offices around the country. The real front line for response however, is the nearly 4,000 standby disaster assistance em- ployees and volunteers who are available for rapid deployment whenever a disaster strikes. FEMA doesn't do the heavy lifting, but works in part- nership with more than 60 state and local emergency centers, 27 fed- eral agencies, the American Red Cross, and many other organizations.

There have been over 1,700 presidentially-declared disasters in the United States since 1953. Each one represents an event that was perceived to be too destructive for state and local governments to man- age without federal assistance. Many of these disasters force residents out of their homes. Residents who choose to remain face the prospect of going days without water, electricity, or energy to cook food or heat their homes, as well as the prospect of contamination and serious injury without the benefit of first aid or appropriate medical care. When individuals in the path of a major storm elect to "ride it out," they are literally taking their lives in their own hands.

Since 1990, FEMA has responded to more than 900 disasters and regional emergencies, including more than 440 since the year 2000.

MOST EXPENSIVE PRESIDENTIALLY-DECLARED DISASTERS

Event	Year	FEMA Funding
Hurricane Katrina Florida, Louisiana, Mississippi, Alabama	2005	$29,318,576,948 **
Attack on America — World Trade Center New York, New Jersey, Virginia	2001	$8,818,350,120
Northridge Earthquake California	1994	$6,978,325,877
Hurricane Rita Texas, Louisiana	2005	$3,749,698,351
Hurricane Ivan Louisiana, Alabama, Mississippi, Florida, North Carolina, Georgia, New Jersey, Pennsylvania, West Virginia, New York, Tennessee	2004	$2,431,034,355
Hurricane Georges Alabama, Florida, Mississippi, Puerto Rico, U.S. Virgin Islands	1998	$2,245,157,178
Hurricane Wilma Florida	2005	$2,110,738,364
Hurricane Charley Florida, South Carolina	2004	$1,885,466,628
Hurricane Andrew Florida, Louisiana	1992	$1,813,594,813
Hurricane Frances Florida, North Carolina, Pennsylvania, Ohio, New York, Georgia, South Carolina	2004	$1,773,440,505

* Numbers are in actual dollars, not adjusted for inflation.
** Approximately 68% funded.

There were 47 Declared Disasters in the year 2005 besides Hurricane Katrina, and another 52 the following year. Every one of these emergencies is a human tragedy, which immediately mobilizes a network of national relief agencies, along with compassionate outreach and aid from dozens of public and private organizations.

A Prophetic Warning

In 2004, several months before the actual disaster, 270 officials from all levels of government participated in a FEMA funded, week-long simulation of a severe hurricane hitting New Orleans. During this exercise, New Orleans officials were told that "the number of people stranded in toxic water may approach 500,000 if residents didn't properly evacuate." When Katrina hit one year later, the truth of that prophetic warning struck home.

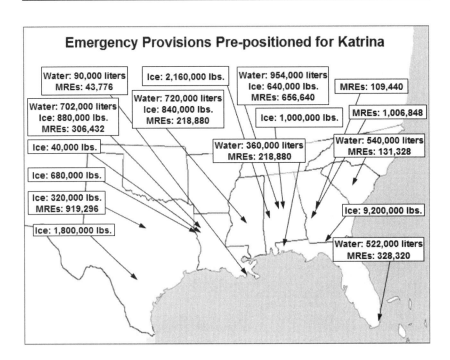

Emergency Provisions Pre-positioned for Katrina

The placement of food, water, and ice in advance of Katrina was the largest pre-positioning of federal emergency provisions in U.S. history. Katrina first made landfall in Florida as a Category 1 hurricane, and didn't come ashore in Louisiana until four days later. In preparation for the Florida landfall, FEMA had pre-staged 100 truckloads of ice, 35 truckloads of food, and seventy truckloads of water.

Then, anticipating a potential second landfall at some point further along the coast, FEMA also pre-staged over 400 truckloads of ice, 500 truckloads of water, and nearly 200 truckloads of pre-packaged meals (MREs) at logistics centers in Alabama, Louisiana, Georgia, Texas, and South Carolina.

Necessities On-Hand Pre-Landfall

The pre-landfall supply of food, water, and ice included 216 trailers with 1,026,432 gallons (3,888,000 liters) of drinking water, 439 trailers with 17,560,000 pounds of ice, and 180 trailers with 3,939,840 Meals Ready to Eat (MREs). FEMA began daily noontime video conference calls on Thursday, August 25 (four days before landfall), which included all federal, state, and local first-responders, to help inform and synchronize the anticipated relief efforts.

As soon as National Hurricane Center storm watchers recognized that Katrina's path was becoming more predictable than usual, NHC Director Max Mayfield issued the most severely worded warning he had ever given in a federal storm warning advisory. The message said:[4]

```
URGENT_WEATHER MESSAGE
NATIONAL WEATHER SERVICE NEW ORLEANS LA
1011 AM CDT SUN AUG 28 2005

... DEVASTATING DAMAGE EXPECTED ...

.HURRICANE KATRINA ... A MOST POWERFUL HURRICANE WITH
UNPRECEDENTED STRENGTH ... RIVALING THE INTENSITY OF HURRI-
CANE CAMILLE OF 1969.

MOST OF THE AREA WILL BE UNINHABITABLE FOR WEEKS ... PERHAPS
LONGER. AT LEAST ONE HALF OF WELL CONSTRUCTED HOMES WILL HAVE
```

ROOF AND WALL FAILURE. ALL GABLED ROOFS WILL FAIL . . . LEAVING THOSE HOMES SEVERELY DAMAGED OR DESTROYED.

THE MAJORITY OF INDUSTRIAL BUILDINGS WILL BECOME NON FUNC-TIONAL. PARTIAL TO COMPLETE WALL AND ROOF FAILURE IS EXPECTED. ALL WOOD FRAMED LOW RISING APARTMENT BUILDINGS WILL BE DESTROYED. CONCRETE BLOCK LOW RISE APARTMENTS WILL SUSTAIN MAJOR DAMAGE . . . INCLUDING SOME WALL AND ROOF FAILURE.

HIGH RISE OFFICE AND APARTMENT BUILDINGS WILL SWAY DANGER-OUSLY . . . A FEW TO THE POINT OF TOTAL COLLAPSE. ALL WINDOWS WILL BLOW OUT.

AIRBORNE DEBRIS WILL BE WIDESPREAD . . . AND MAY INCLUDE HEAVY ITEMS SUCH AS HOUSEHOLD APPLIANCES AND EVEN LIGHT VEHICLES. SPORT UTILITY VEHICLES AND LIGHT TRUCKS WILL BE MOVED. THE BLOWN DEBRIS WILL CREATE ADDITIONAL DESTRUCTION. PERSONS . . . PETS . . . AND LIVESTOCK EXPOSED TO THE WINDS WILL FACE CERTAIN DEATH IF STRUCK.

POWER OUTAGES WILL LAST FOR WEEKS . . . AS MOST POWER POLES WILL BE DOWN AND TRANSFORMERS DESTROYED. WATER SHORTAGES WILL MAKE HUMAN SUFFERING INCREDIBLE BY MODERN STANDARDS.

THE VAST MAJORITY OF NATIVE TREES WILL BE SNAPPED OR UPROOTED. ONLY THE HEARTIEST WILL REMAIN STANDING . . . BUT BE TOTALLY DEFO-LIATED. FEW CROPS WILL REMAIN. LIVESTOCK LEFT EXPOSED TO THE WINDS WILL BE KILLED.

AN INLAND HURRICANE WIND WARNING IS ISSUED WHEN SUSTAINED WINDS NEAR HURRICANE FORCE . . . OR FREQUENT GUSTS AT OR ABOVE HURRICANE FORCE . . . ARE CERTAIN WITHIN THE NEXT 12 TO 24 HOURS.

ONCE TROPICAL STORM AND HURRICANE FORCE WINDS ONSET . . . DO NOT VENTURE OUTSIDE!

---

[4] National Oceanic and Atmospheric Administration website http://www.srh .noaa.gov/data/warn_archive/LIX/NPW/0828_155101.txt

On Saturday, FEMA's Region IV and VI headquarters in Atlanta and Denton, Texas, respectively, commenced "Level 1 Operations," requiring full-staffing around the clock, seven days a week. FEMA Region VI dis-patched its Mobile Emergency Response Support (MERS) detachment to Camp Beauregard, Louisiana, and requested the deployment of another MERS unit all the way from Denver to Denton, Texas, to serve as backup. On Saturday afternoon, shelters began opening throughout the region, and state emergency management agencies began deploying FEMA supplies to them, including the New Orleans Superdome. At Camp Beauregard, Region VI had staged 270,000 liters of water (71,280 gallons), 680,000 pounds of ice, 15,120 tarps, and 328,320 MREs. By 5:00 P.M., the quantity of water stored at Camp Beauregard had doubled to 140,000 gallons. Also on Saturday, FEMA began activating the National Disaster Medical System (NDMS), Disaster Medical Assistance Teams (DMATs), and Urban Search and Rescue (US&R) teams.

On Saturday evening, President Bush signed a Federal Emergency Declaration for the state of Louisiana, in response to the official request by Governor Blanco. On Sunday, he signed similar emergency declarations for Mississippi and Alabama. The issuance of a presidential emergency declaration before landfall is extremely rare; it has only been done once since 1990. By signing these declarations, the president not only signaled the extreme urgency, he directed the federal government to provide full assistance to the residents of the stricken area to save lives and property—in advance.

In another unprecedented move, the director of the National Hurricane Center called Governor Blanco to make a personal plea that residents be warned and evacuated. This was the only time he had made such a call in his 36 year career.

Closing Saturday's noontime video teleconference with his regional staff and the State EOCs, FEMA director Michael Brown urged all attendees to put forth an extra effort with unusually strong language:

I know I'm preaching to the choir on this one, but I've learned over the past four and a half, five years, to go with my gut on a lot of things, and I've got to tell you my gut hurts with this one. It hurts. . . . So we need to take this one very, very seriously. . . . I want you guys to lean forward as far as possible. . . . Why is this important? Because I worry about the people in New Orleans, Louisiana, and Mississippi right now, and they're going to need our help.

The first Emergency Response Team leader arrived in Baton Rouge, Louisiana, on Saturday evening. On Sunday morning, 3 FEMA State Liaison Officers were deployed to the three gulf coast states. Also, early on Sunday morning, President Bush called Governor Blanco to urge that mandatory evacuation orders be issued for New Orleans, again signaling an unusual sense of urgency—he was on vacation at the time. After that call, Mayor Ray Nagin and Governor Blanco held a press conference during which the Mayor ordered a mandatory evacuation.

At noon on Sunday, the President participated in the FEMA conference call with Michael Brown and NHC Director Max Mayfield, and personally encouraged state and local officials to use precaution and get the word out to their citizens. He offered the full support and resources of the federal government. Then after the noon conference, the President issued a nationally covered public statement saying, "We cannot stress enough the danger this hurricane poses to Gulf Coast communities. I urge all citizens to put their own safety and the safety of their families first by moving to safe ground."

It was not until after the call from President Bush on Sunday that Mayor Nagin decided to order a mandatory evacuation. However, the buses designated for the purpose sat idle while the punch bowl that was New Orleans filled up with water. Ironically, the shrillest complaints about FEMA's response later on were that not enough buses arrived fast enough.[5]

By Sunday evening thousands of people were streaming into 114 shelters with space and supplies for over 28,000 people. Federal, state and local governments had worked with the Red Cross and other non-profit organizations to make these preparations. The Superdome, which was originally intended to shelter only the special needs population (elderly, sick, immobile), was unfortunately changed to a "shelter of last resort" for the general population, and later became a free-for-all when Mayor Nagin asserted in a press conference that the Superdome could accommodate 50,000 to 70,000 people.

The Louisiana National Guard had pre-positioned about 10,000 MREs (meals) and over 13,000 bottles of water at the Superdome. At noon on Sunday, as Katrina approached, officials requested an additional 180,000 liters (47,520 gallons) of water and 109,000 meals for the Superdome. Amazingly, FEMA was able to distribute an additional 90,000 liters of water and 43,000 meals before high winds forced the trucks to turn back.

In addition to stocking the Superdome, the Louisiana National Guard sent additional personnel to the Superdome throughout the day on Sunday. A 46-member Special Reaction Team—a unit "highly trained in law enforcement missions"—arrived at 7 A.M. By 3 P.M., the 527th Ready Reaction Force had arrived with 220 crowd control personnel. The 225th Engineering Group joined that evening with 220 soldiers to "assist with security." Another 100 personnel from the 159th Fighter Wing also came to assist with security. Additional medical personnel from the National Guard also arrived to assist at the Superdome. Five physicians, 4 nurses, 20 medics, and 6 Managed Care Organizations (MCOs) were added to supplement those already in place. Altogether, 71 medical personnel were on hand by the time the hurricane struck.

"If anyone rioted, it was the media."
—*From the Bipartisan Report*

By Thursday morning, conditions in the Superdome were atrocious. It was sheltering a population many times what was intended and as a result restroom facilities were inadequate. The unlucky souls who found themselves in those conditions wanted out and, as one would expect, lines started to form as soon as word got around that there were busses on their way to take them away.

With nothing to do but stand and wait in long lines, it is easy to understand why false rumors spread about the imminent arrival of more buses. For hours on end the unfulfilled expectations added to the frustration and the seeming incompetence of those who had supposedly promised them. These rumors, and similarly false ones about rapes in the Superdome and unbridled killing in the city, were seized upon by the media as evidence of wanton chaos.

Reports in the press claimed that as many as 100 had died in the Superdome, mostly from heat exhaustion. Another report held that an accused rapist had been beaten to death by a crowd. The actual death toll in the Superdome was six—four from natural causes, one overdose, and an apparent suicide.[6]

The media's role in the Katrina disaster hasn't been overlooked entirely. A bipartisan congressional report released in February 2006 accuses the media of making a bad situation worse. In their investigation of FEMA's preparations for and responses to Hurricane Katrina, researchers found that the media's claims that gunshots had been fired at rescue helicopters were false. And the sensational reports of rioting in the streets were, if not false, unsubstantiated and overstated. Unfortunately, as a result of these reports, relief personnel from the Red Cross and federal troops were given orders not to go into areas that were perceived as dangerous—where the need for help was so great.

In their final assessment of issues reported by the media that stirred millions of Americans to fear, shock, and outrage during those long and troublesome weeks, they concluded by saying, "Clear accurate reporting was among Katrina's many victims. If anyone rioted, it was the media."

Assessment

How amazing is this country? Consider the incredible list of things done by all levels of government and volunteers, from predicting the storm, warning people, conducting preparedness exercises, positioning emergency provisions, dropping 3,000 pound sand bags, rescuing people, transporting them, feeding them, sheltering them, providing medical assistance and local leadership, arranging emergency evacuation road schemes, providing emergency living allowances, and even providing heroic on-site journalistic coverage. How is it possible that when someone says Katrina today, the reflex rejoinder is "government incompetence."

In early 2008, the death toll from a Typhoon in Myanmar reportedly passed 70,000. The death toll from Katrina, which was not just a hurricane but also the total deluge of a city, was 1,351.[7]

Were mistakes made? Yes. The worst mistake seems have been the failure to use the city's buses to evacuate the people despite the most repeated and emphatic warnings ever in advance of a disaster. Second would be sensational reporting of the press, which seriously hampered the relief efforts, most notably of the Red Cross. The worst by FEMA seems to be the failure to have interoperable communication systems.[8]

One cannot read the accounts above and conclude that our elected officials at the federal level did not care what happened in New Orleans.

If anyone wants to understand how some in the press think about the way the world works, consider the following quote from author and professor Douglas Brinkley, son of journalist David Brinkley, in his book *The Great Deluge*, about Katrina:

> Around nightfall Governor Blanco was in a helicopter flying over the Louisiana devastation. She refused to let a couple of pool reporters come with her. Her lack of media savvy proved to be a serious Achilles heel. Only 'lifesaving people can go out,' she scolded the press. That was her prerogative. It was also the media's prerogative to stick a knife so deep in her back that even Karl Rove winced.

If you find the account of events in this chapter to be at odds with what you have heard in the press about the response to Katrina, and if you admire people who would rather do something than just watch by while the press "sticks a knife in" the back of others with whom they have a bone to pick—including that of the U.S. president—please recommend this book broadly. Spreading truth and setting the record straight about your country is worth a few minutes of your time.

14

Social Security Sinking

CONVENTIONAL WISDOM

Social Security is not really in trouble. The politicians just want to cut back on what the government owes retirees.

Typical Headlines

"Americans Skeptical About Social Security Crisis"
—*CNN, Apr. 10, 1998*

"What Crisis?: It Ain't Broke, So No Need To Fix It"
—*Washington Post, Jan. 23, 2005*

"Social Security Problems Not a Crisis, Most Say"
—*Washington Post, Feb. 10, 2005*

Facts

Both Social Security and Medicare are funded by taxes withheld from salaries and wages. Workers pay 6.2% for Social Security up to $94,200 in earnings and another 1.45% for Medicare on all of their earnings. Their employers then match those amounts. The self-employed pay

15.3% of earnings for both programs, but then get to deduct the employer portion on their tax return.

The debate over how to make Social Security solvent for the long-term has apparently been put on hold, while the debates over how to address the larger and more immediate shortfalls in Medicare haven't even begun in earnest in Washington. But it's highly likely that corrective measures will include one or both of the following: tax increases and benefit reductions.

By 2030, there will be 84 million people on Social Security in this country, up 68% from the 50 million men and women currently on the government's rolls. At the same time, Medicare will go from 44 million beneficiaries to more than 79 million. The reason for this jump is that the proverbial "pig in the python," the Baby Boomer Generation, is reaching retirement age, which means that the Social Security system will be facing an estimated $50 trillion obligation over the next 75 years.

According to figures provided by the annual Trustees Report, the Social Security system will go from 4% to 6% of the nation's economy, and Medicare will go from 3% to 11%. One expert observes that the impending crisis in Social Security and Medicare will soon be "the single greatest economic challenge of our era." Already, Medicare's hospital insurance fund pays out more than it is taking in.

Projections show that the Medicare insurance fund will be out of business by 2019 unless Congress begins taking this challenge seriously. Social Security will go into deficit spending by the year 2017 and will be fully bankrupt by 2041.[1] Waiting even one year to begin solving this problem will add an additional $600 billion to the price tag.

Assessment

During his Saturday radio address on January 15, 2005, President Bush told the nation, "If we do not act now, government will eventually be left with two choices: dramatically reduce benefits or impose a massive, economically ruinous tax increase. Leaving our children with such a mess would be a generational betrayal."[2] We've been warned.

The President took bold steps to try and address this problem early in his second term, but was blocked by Democrats in Congress and the mass media. The President had the courage to stand squarely on the third rail, but rather than deal with the problem and confront the risks facing older Americans, the United States Congress and the mass media turned away, and turned on the switch.

Organized Dissent

President Bush alerted the nation to what was happening in his 2005 State of the Union Address, saying that the path we're on today is "headed toward bankruptcy." He didn't attempt to dictate policy or pressure Congress to follow his script. Rather, he said that, "Fixing Social Security permanently will require an open, candid review of the options," meaning that both sides of the aisle were invited to weigh in and offer options for fixing the problem.

In a scripted response to those remarks, however, the Democratic Minority Leader in the Senate, Harry Reid, said, "We so strongly disagree with the president's plan to privatize Social Security." His party, Reid said, would prefer for government to make all the investment decisions. He said, "The Bush plan isn't really Social Security reform; it's more like Social Security roulette. Democrats are all for giving Americans more of a say, and more choices when it comes to their retirement savings, but that doesn't mean taking Social Security's guarantee and gambling with it."

From that moment on, there was an orchestrated chorus of boos from liberal politicians and media pundits all across America. In an opinion editorial published in *BusinessWeek*, economist Laura D'Andrea Tyson, a former Clinton administration economist, wrote, "For nearly 70 years, Social Security has provided all working Americans with a basic level of income protected against inflation, financial market fluctuations, not to mention the risks of disability, losing a family wage-earner, or outliving one's assets. With a few modest changes, it can continue to deliver this remarkable security." And she concluded by saying, "There is no crisis."[3]

At the same time, *New York Times* columnist Paul Krugman told a *Rolling Stone* reporter that it would be years before anyone needs to worry about the coming bankruptcy of the Social Security system. "If you're twenty now, you'll be hitting retirement around 2052," he said. "That's the year the Congressional Budget Office says the trust fund will run out. In fact, many economists say it may never run out." Short of denying the risks, however, Krugman added that, "if the trust fund is ever depleted, then something will have to be done. . . . On the day the trust fund is exhausted, Social Security revenue will cover about 80% of the cost of benefits."

Where does this sort of denial eventually lead? Instead of taking steps to fix the problem now, so retirees can actually anticipate receiving 100% of their Social Security benefits, Krugman, Tyson, and other Democrats said they would prefer to wait and see what happens. The problem is that many on that side don't trust average Americans to make their own decisions about how their retirement funds ought to be invested. Government, they believe, can do it better.[4]

AARP's Assessment of the Alternatives

The American Association of Retired Persons (AARP) certainly has a vested interest in the future of Social Security and Medicare, and devoted a great deal of space in their publications to the various proposals. Even though the AARP generally advocates socially liberal policies and tends to support predominantly Democratic perspectives, their researchers have warned that taking no action will mean leaving current tax laws as they are but, over time, pushing all taxpayers into higher and higher tax brackets.

The AARP's 2007 report on aging and entitlements notes that the Congressional Budget Office (CBO) regularly analyzes several long-term budget scenarios to determine the sustainability of entitlement spending. In these scenarios, the most important cost factor is the projected growth of health care costs, and the most important revenue element is whether or not Congress takes action to raise or lower taxes.

The intermediate scenario considered by the CBO assumes that Medicare and Medicaid will grow at a rate of one percentage point faster than the rate of growth of per capita GDP. By this standard, Medicare and Medicaid spending would triple from 4.2% of GDP in 2005 to 12.6% in 2050. Consequently, the three largest entitlements would more than double from 8.4% to 19% of GDP over the same period. Total federal spending, then, would rise by 50%, from 20.1% to 30% of GDP. Further, spending entitlements would rise as a share of federal primary (non-interest) spending from 45% to 75% between 2005 and 2050.

On the revenue side, CBO's revenue scenarios followed one of two rules of thumb: First, take no action and keep things as they are; or, second, change the law to keep revenues at the same ratio to GDP that they have been for the past 30 years (about 18.3%). The first option requires no congressional action, but the second requires periodic tax cuts. The "no action" approach, coupled with continued growth of health spending, would mean a primary deficit between revenues and primary spending of 1.6% of GDP by the year 2050.

The reports add further that, while Social Security is out of actuarial balance, the reforms needed to bring it back to balance are not radical. Social Security has a financing gap equal to roughly 2% of covered payroll to make it solvent for the next 75 years. And the AARP report concludes that it's unlikely that solvency can be achieved with revenue-only or spending-only solutions.[5] The point being that the findings of this liberal advocacy group disagree strongly with the conclusions of Democrat leaders in Congress who oppose Social Security reform.

While AARP's analysts support the idea of raising taxes across the board to restore balance in these vital systems, the Bush administration plans would have cut taxes to encourage growth and expand revenues, thus increasing overall GDP and increasing contributions to the trust fund. At the same time, younger taxpayers would have been given the option of investing a portion of their income tax-free, matched with government funds, in individual retirement accounts that would help take care of their future needs.

The Trustees Report for 2007

Despite strong warnings from the White House and supporting documentation from dozens of federal agencies and private research groups, pressure from congressional Democrats and the mass media have at least temporarily stopped the President's reform package in its tracks. Yet, year after year, as Mr. Bush has said, the system continues to slide backward, and the evidence that Social Security and Medicare will one day collapse from lack of funding keeps mounting.

In their 2007 Report, issued two years after the President's speech, the trustees wrote, "The financial condition of the Social Security and Medicare programs remains problematic; we believe their currently projected long run growth rates are not sustainable under current financing arrangements. Medicare's Hospital Insurance (HI) Trust Fund is already expected to pay out more in hospital benefits this year than it receives in taxes and other dedicated revenues.

"The growing annual deficits in both programs," they said, "are projected to exhaust HI reserves in 2019 and Social Security reserves in 2041. In addition, the Medicare Supplementary Medical Insurance (SMI) Trust Fund that pays for physician services and the new prescription drug benefit will continue to require general revenue financing and charges on beneficiaries that grow faster than the economy and beneficiary incomes over time."

As the trustees had reported the previous year, Medicare's financial difficulties will come sooner—and are potentially much more severe—than those confronting Social Security at the moment. While both programs face demographic challenges, the impact will be substantially greater for Medicare because health care costs are increasing, and they grow larger as individuals grow older. Health care costs per enrollee, they said, are projected to rise faster than the wages of workers still actively paying into the system. "As a result," they've warned, "while Medicare's annual costs were 3.1% of GDP in 2006, or about 72% of Social Security's, they are projected to surpass Social Security expenditures in 2028 and exceed 11% of GDP in 2081."

DEFINITIONS OF KEY TERMS

OASDI	Old Age, Survivors And Disability Insurance
OASI	Old Age, Survivors Insurance
DI	Disability Insurance
HI	Medicare Hospitality Insurance
SMI	Medicare Supplementary Insurance includes PART B Physician Services and Part D New Medicare Drug Benefit

Based on the current situation, the trustees were required to trigger what they term a Medicare Funding Warning, which requires the President to propose legislation that responds to this situation within fifteen days of the submission of the Fiscal Year 2009 budget. Simultaneously, the warning requires Congress to consider the President's proposal for repairing the Social Security and Medicare systems on an expedited basis.

The Chart below shows the amount of total US GDP that will have to be redirected to cover the costs of Social Security and Medicare if nothing is changed. Medicare and Social Security costs are projected to grow substantially faster than the economy over the next several decades, but unless current laws are changed, tax income that supports the HI and OASDI Trust Funds will not grow fast enough to help. Because the primary source of income for HI and OASDI is the payroll tax, it is customary to compare the programs' income and costs expressed as percentages of taxable payroll.

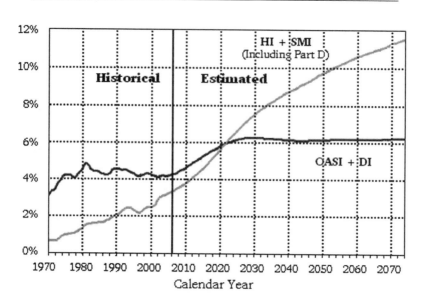

Social Security and Medicare Cost as a percentage of GDP

Income and Cost Rates

The data demonstrates that payroll taxes would have to be 30% of all salaries in order to cover Social Security and Medicare costs in 2050. In other words, it would require a tax of almost a third of pay for all workers just to cover the Old Age, Survivors and Disability Insurance as well as the Medicare Hospitality Insurance and and Supplementary insurance including Part B and D. The gap between total non-interest income and expenditures steadily widens for Social Security, due to growing annual HI (Health Insurance) deficits, which will reach 3.4% of GDP by 2081. All told, by 2081 the Medicare program is projected to require SMI (Supplementary Medical Insurance) general revenue transfers equal to 4.7% of GDP. Moreover, the HI deficit added to that would total 8.1% of GDP, and there is no provision to address this deficit under current law through general tax revenue transfers or any other means.

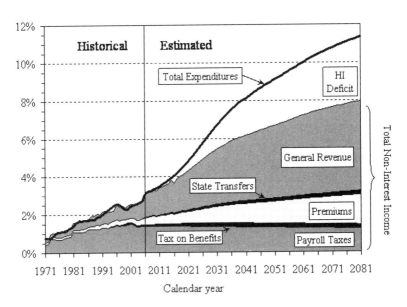

Medicare Expenditures and Non-Interest Income by Source as a percent of GDP

To put these magnitudes into historical perspective, in 2006 the combined annual cost of HI, SMI, and OASDI amounted to 40% of total federal revenues, or about 7% of GDP. That cost (as a percentage of GDP) is projected to double by 2042, and then increase to nearly 18% of GDP in 2081. It is noteworthy that over the past four decades, the average amount of total federal revenues as a percentage of GDP has also been 18%, and has never exceeded 21% in a given year. Assuming the continued need to fund a wide range of other government functions, the projected growth in Social Security and Medicare costs would require that the total Federal revenue share of GDP increase to unprecedented levels and taxes would eventually rise to fund that expense.

The Social Security Administration base case, which underlies all this data, assumes long term GDP growth of 2.8%, 1 million (legal)

immigrants per year, productivity growth averaging 1.6%, and steady births per woman of 1.95. If any of these numbers were actually higher it would reduce the Social Security deficit. Lower numbers would increase the deficit. More workers and faster GDP growth obviously lead to more income to the Social Security Trust Fund. The Social Security Administration also assumes average hourly earnings growth of 3.9% per year and an average annual CPI increase of 3.8%. Clearly higher inflation and faster wage growth, to which Social Security payouts are indexed, would increase the deficit. If unemployment rate were higher than the assumed 5.5%, this would also increase the deficit because there would be fewer workers contributing to the Trust Fund. Although there is no certainty about any of these assumptions, they are fair and reasonable.

These numbers do not indicate that there is a crisis today, but they predict certain bankruptcy and either a failure to fulfill the promised benefits to young people currently in the workforce, or a crippling future tax burden. This is why the Social Security Trust Fund administrators have been required by law to issue a formal warning.

Even if they do not support administration reform proposals, the AARP nevertheless agreed that the current situation is unsustainable, and their report examines possible choices for finding balance based on their own assumptions. The association's assumptions take Congressional Budget Office projections (which assume slightly lower growth in health care costs and a stronger GDP growth than the Trust Fund's assumptions, and the AARP analysts also assume no change is made to tax laws, implying we all move to higher tax brackets. They also assume even more moderation in health care costs, which is certainly not a controllable option.

It's interesting that an institution such as the AARP is against allowing individuals to use a small percentage of the Social Security payroll tax to invest in programs of their choice, and yet they propose as a reasonable option that government could solve 48% of the deficit problem by "investing in the stock market." In other words, it is not

SOCIAL SECURITY SOLVENCY OPTIONS

OPTIONS	SSA ESTIMATES: PERCENT OF LONG-TERM (75 YEAR) DEFICIT RESOLVED
Across-the-Board Tax and Benefit Measures	
Immediately raise payroll tax rates from 12.4% to 14.3%	100%
Immediately reduce benefits by 13%	100%
Cost-of-Living Adjustment (COLA) Options	
Reduce Consumer Price Index by 0.5% annually	36%
Reduce Consumer Price Index by 1.0% annually	69%
Change the Benefit Calculation Formula	
Index earnings to price inflation instead of wage inflation	112%
Add a third bendpoint: new bendpoints at $580, $725, and $3,381; new rates at 90%, 50%, 25%, and 12%	25%
Increase number of work years used in benefit calculation from 35 to 38	11%
Raise the Normal Retirement Age (NRA)	
Raise the NRA to age 68	20%
Raise the NRA to age 70	26%
Taxation of Benefits	
Tax Social Security benefits like private pensions and put revenue in trust funds	17%
Adjust the Taxable Maximum (maximum amount of wages or salaries subject to payroll tax	
Make 90% of earnings subject to payroll tax and credit them for benefit calculations	29%
Other Options	
Cover all newly hired state and local government employees	11%
Invest 40% of trust fund assets in stocks	48%

SOURCE: ARC-AARP SOCIAL SECURITY SOLVENCY MODEL

appropriate for the beneficiaries of the Social Security system to invest their own money in federally approved programs, but it's perfectly acceptable if government does it for them.

The logic is perplexing, but whichever way the debate goes from here, something needs to happen, and the "condemn and suppress" approach being taken by Congress at present isn't helping. Government statistics show that, for a third of all Americans over 65, Social Security provides over 90% of their income. This figure isn't likely to change over time, which means that for everyone's future well-being, it's very important to prevent the system from collapsing.

The Administration Proposal

1. No one born before 1950 will be affected by the change; they will continue under current system.
2. Any idea other than raising payroll taxes can be considered.
3. Younger workers would be allowed to put up to 4% of their payroll taxes into private investment accounts.
4. Funds invested could only go into a limited set of bond and stock accounts.
5. This plan would reduce the future liability for the Social Security Trust.

In 1950 there were 16 workers per beneficiary. Currently there are only 3.3 workers per beneficiary, and that number is continuing to fall, making the system unsustainable. President Bush has said that all ideas are on the table, and the administration is eager to look into any reasonable option to resolve the Social Security dilemma.

Administration proposals would allow workers to voluntarily direct some of their payroll taxes into a separate investment account. Under this scenario, each worker would have true ownership of his or her own money, and they would benefit from the results of their investments when they retire. Furthermore, they would be able to pass those funds on to their children if they don't use them. This plan would increase deficits in the near term, because it will be recognizing future deficits earlier in order to reduce future payouts. And, perhaps most important of all, the plan is also logical and practical, and deserves to have a fairer hearing than it has been given so far.

15

Sub Prime Simplified

CONVENTIONAL WISDOM

The housing situation is a complete disaster and will just continue its downward spiral.

Typical Headlines

"Housing Prices to Free Fall in 2008–Merrill"
—*CNNMoney.com, Jan. 23, 2008*

"Probing the Depth of the Downturn:
Market Volatility Expected to Continue"
—*Washington Post, Nov. 11, 2007*

"Home-loan defaults spread to lower-risk borrowers"
—*Times Online, Mar. 5, 2007*

Facts

Since the end of World War II, the growth of the American middle class has mirrored the growth in home ownership. From the 1960s into the 1990s, home ownership remained stable at about 64% of all households.[1] Then, beginning in 1995, the volume of home ownership began increasing steadily, and peaked at 69.2% during 2004 and 2005. Interestingly, most of this dramatic increase in home ownership actually came before the increase in so-called "sub prime mortgages."

However, even if prices were to drop another 10%, the value of the average home would still be up 40% from the level set in 2000, as measured by the Case Schiller Home Price Index.

The only homeowners currently experiencing serious depreciation compared to the purchase price of their property are those who bought homes in 2005 or 2006. Unfortunately, the peak in the housing market in 2005 and 2006 was also the peak in home buyers' use of high levels of leveraged borrowing. Many individuals who stretched their budgets to buy expensive homes with large mortgages were simply unable to keep up with the payments over the long term. And many who had taken out Adjustable Rate Mortgages (ARM) with substantially higher payments after a two- to three-year introductory period suddenly found that with the payment resets their mortgages were taking most of their income.

Housing in Context

The real story of the recent sub prime crisis is, in fact, another sad example of the unanticipated consequences of government's meddling in the economy. The potential for a sub prime disaster was created in the late 1990s by legislation requiring banks to lend to individuals who would not have qualified for a traditional home loan. Bowing to pressure from grassroots lobbying organizations, and ignoring the strong resistance of the banking industry as well as members of the House and Senate banking committees, Congress passed and President Clinton signed the Community Reinvestment Act (CRA) of 1997, which required lenders to extend credit to "underserved members of the community" who might not otherwise qualify for a loan.

The CRA also required each lending institution to be evaluated on a regular basis to ensure that it was paying attention to "the credit needs of its entire community." Faced with the requirement to make risky loans, however, many lending institutions decided to "securitize" these transactions. That is, rather than keeping the loans on their own books and potentially weakening their financial position, the original lenders simply charged a fee for services and sold these notes to other banks and mortgage lenders.

The result of buyers stretching to pay high home prices in 2005 and 2006 led directly and predictably to the rapid expansion in the sub prime market. By that time the average home price had become too high for individuals with average incomes to qualify for traditional prime mortgages. The Index of Housing Affordability, which normally averages between 130 and 140, had dropped to 100. This meant that home prices were more than 30% higher than normal when compared to median family household income. Consequently, the mortgage payments on these sub prime mortgages were unmanageable. Even in good times, sub prime loans have a significantly higher rate of default and foreclosure than normal prime loans. But under the induced pressure of government mandates and surveillance, lenders began engaging in practices that would prove to be destructive to bank credit and implode many individual loans.

Even though home prices were continuing to rise in 2006 and 2007, the handwriting was on the wall. The rating agencies that gave out the AAA ratings on packages of these Sub Prime loans never actually owned a mortgage. They merely gave an opinion that with the right structure, and based on lending history, the risk of actually losing money was low. The hedge funds and Structured Investment Vehicles (SIV) that had bought these "securitized" loan portfolios had unbalanced incentives because they earned huge returns when the investments made money. The fund managers and companies that ran these vehicles kept 20% of the profits on the portfolios of loans, but all the losses went to their investors.

Case Schiller Home Price Index

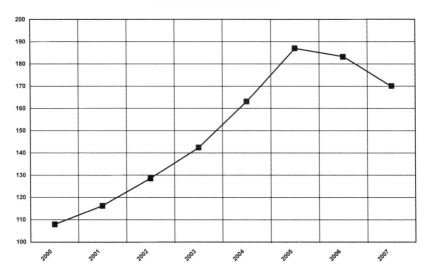

Housing has been a winner for the vast majority of Americans, and even after the recent price drop, most homes are worth more than their original purchase price. The Case Schiller home price index, shown above, is still up 50% from the level in 2000, and the median home price is up 30% over that period. However, as the mortgage crisis unfolded in early 2008, home ownership dropped to 67.8%, meaning that many of the individuals designated by Congress as the "underserved" were suddenly in over their heads. And many would have to make some dramatic adjustments in their living arrangements.

The Mortgage Crunch

The most serious losses in the recent mortgage crunch have fallen on those with adjustable rate mortgages (ARM). After a predetermined period of time—generally 2 to 3 years—these rates reset at an above-market rate, to make up for the lower revenues to the lender during the introductory period. In many cases these were the "underserved borrowers" for whom banks had created products to bring them into home ownership. But for many, the new product turned into a "poisoned apple" of credit destruction. Some of these borrowers expected that increasing home values or improved individual finances would enable them to pay off their expensive mortgages before the rates reset and get a better deal. But when home prices began falling, it became all too obvious that those better deals weren't going to be available.

The overall delinquency rate on all home mortgages Prime and Sub Prime has gone up from less than 2% in 2005 to nearly 4% in 2007, and the rate continues to rise to 6.35% in the first quarter of 2008.[2] Eventually delinquency, being late by more than 30 days on your mortgage payment, must be cured by making up missed payments or the bank will protect its cash flow by foreclosing on the house and selling it. Sub prime ARMs went from a foreclosure rate of 3% in 2005 to almost 8% in early 2008, while sub prime fixed rate mortgages (FRM) remained steady at a little over 3% foreclosure rate. The housing markets that had experienced the greatest price appreciation are now witnessing the greatest drop in value. Those who bought at the peak and borrowed 90% of the cost of their new home have discovered that the mortgages they're obligated to pay are larger than the price for which they can sell the home.

In such situations, new financing will not be available unless the borrower can pay off a considerable amount of the mortgage, to bring the amount of the debt down to the new lower value of the home. However, the vast majority of sub prime borrowers simply can't afford to do that. So the result is a higher than normal level of delinquencies, which soon turns into a higher rate of foreclosures.

Risky Business

As the first shockwaves of the sub prime crisis began to rattle windows on Wall Street and in independent banking and lending institutions around the country, there was a sudden flurry of activity, both at the national and local levels, to try and head off a potential disaster. The state attorneys general of 36 states came together to create a team to collect data from the mortgage service companies to analyze the problem. After looking into all the issues, the State Foreclosure Prevention Working Group issued its report in October 2007, which concluded that in reality very few borrowers were on track to mitigate the impact of the delinquency, payment resets were not driving the increase in delinquencies, and the option to refinance with a new loan had evaporated.

A Joint Economic Committee report issued in October 2007 confirmed that the criteria for lenders to make new mortgage loans had deteriorated over the last few years, making loans more risky to lenders and borrowers alike. Since 2003, the number of ARM loans increased from 80% to 90% of all sub prime loans. To make the problem even more complex, as the ARM share was increasing "Interest Only" and "Low-or-No Doc" loans were increasing as well. This means that many borrowers had loans for which they were paying only interest on the mortgage and no principal, while many others who could not actually document their incomes were approved for loans they could not prove they could afford.

In the last few years of the housing boom, and as lending criteria became irrationally lenient, the vast majority of new mortgages were "securitized." That is, the loans were made by lenders who had no intention of taking the actual risk, and didn't plan on sticking around to see if the borrowers could actually pay off their loans. As soon as the loans were completed, they were packaged with other loans and sold to investors who had no close relationship to the borrower, and no in-depth knowledge of the details of the loans they were buying.

These buyers wanted to earn a higher than market interest rate, and they took the risk. The mortgages in these securitized transactions were packaged in many ways and often distributed to leveraged buyers, such as hedge funds or off-balance-sheet subsidiaries of banks.

The share of sub prime loans securitized in this way went from 50% of all sub prime home loans in 2004 to over 80% in 2007. Clearly, the lending institutions were getting these loans off their books as quickly as possible. But the risks for the lenders and borrowers were compounding faster than anyone could imagine.

Getting in Deeper

Adding another layer of complexity to the impending collapse, the lending institution of Bear Stearns (now defunct), along with others, added a new layer of financial leverage by creating instruments they called KLIOS.[3] In these arrangements, a separate entity was set up by the bank with equity investors who were supposed to receive very high returns on their capital. The bank provided a "liquidity put" (a negotiated investment agreement) for Money Market lenders who made short term loans to the KLIO.

With the equity investor taking the risk of the first losses and the bank guaranteeing liquidity to short term lenders, these creations were easily able to borrow vast sums of money from Money Market investors who never looked at the underlying investments in AA and AAA blocks of Collateralized Debt Obligations (CDO). The banks had provided the "liquidity put" because they believed the collateral was all AAA. They earned high fees and could even sell their sub prime mortgage pools into the entity creating a "riskless" revenue stream.

If all of this sounds terribly complex, that's because it is. And the lack of clarity in the system was part of what brought everything to a crashing halt in 2008. In 2004 and 2005, Bear Stearns had set up $10 billion worth of KLIOS. The KLIO structure was very profitable, and before long other institutions were copying the structure in the form of SIVs (Structured Investment Vehicles). This all looked very attractive to the banks. With the right equity structure, they could earn interest on tens of billions of dollars in investments without having to record them on the balance sheet, and they didn't even have to set aside capital for the investments. A thin layer of capital from investors was layered with bank loans so that as little as $100 million of capital was buying $2 billion worth of mortgages.*

So how big was this off-balance-sheet structuring? The asset backed commercial paper market was the primary funding vehicle for these entities. From outstanding balances of $500 billion in 2005, asset backed commercial paper boomed to $1.2 trillion by the middle of 2007. In just two years, the amount of asset backed paper expanded $700 billion at a time when about $1 trillion worth of sub prime mortgages were securitized. The asset-backed commercial paper market was also supporting other types of assets besides sub prime, but the sub prime securitization was a big part of it.

What Really Happened?

In 2005–2006, despite rising home prices, sub prime delinquencies and foreclosures started to climb. By early 2007, the housing price indexes all started to show declining prices, particularly in some of the hottest urban and suburban markets. The owners of CDOs started to worry as prices dropped.[4] The lower credit piece of CDO securities, after having traded for years in the high 90s close to the par 100 level that would indicate 100% of the loan would be repaid, suddenly

---

* A useful definition of Klio Funding is provided by Peter Cohan, who writes that a KLIO is an entity that sells short-term loans, then uses the revenue to buy higher-yielding longer term investments. According to Yale University economist Robert J. Shiller, the Klio structure turns out to be a gigantic pyramid scheme. As each new investor enters the picture, they bring new cash and cause prices to rise, boosting the profits for those who bought in earlier. The bigger the profits, the more investors will want to get in on the action. Thus, the scheme continue, until one or more participants decides to take out a substantial amount of their money. For details, see Peter Cohan, "Bear Stearns and Klio Funding," BloggingStocks.com, Dec. 20, 2007. [http://www.bloggingstocks.com/2007/12/20/bears-bear-boosts-bust/] (accessed Apr. 28, 2008).

Mortage Origination Statistics

Mortgage Origination Statistics					
	Total Mortgage Originations ($ Billions)	Subprime Originations ($ Billions)	Subprime Share in Total Originations (percent of dollar value)	Subprime Mortgage Backed Securities ($ Billions)	Percent Subprimes Securitized (percent of dollar value)
2001	2,215	190	8.6	95	50.4
2002	2,885	231	8.0	121	52.7
2003	3,945	335	8.5	202	60.5
2004	2,920	540	18.5	401	74.3
2005	3,120	625	20.0	507	81.2
2006	2,980	600	20.1	483	80.5
Source: Inside Mortgage Finance. The 2007 Mortgage Market Statistical Annual. Top Subprime Mortgage Market Players and Key Data (2006).					

Bear Stearns, CDO, SIV, and the alphabet soup of a credit crunch.

started to trade in the mid 60 price range that implied 40% loss on the loans. The bell had been rung, and investors started to wake up and examine the assets underlying the sub prime market and the risks involved.

By late 2007, increasing foreclosures had caused investors to fear what could happen to the KLIO and SIV structures. The asset backed commercial paper market shrank rapidly as money market investors refused to roll over investments in the off-balance-sheet companies. From $1.2 trillion in mid 2007, asset-backed commercial paper out-standing dropped to under $800 billion by the end of 2007. Banks were forced to take assets back on to their balance sheets and hedge funds were forced to hold "fire sales" to liquidate investments loaded up with sub prime asset backed CDO securities.

Recent, 2007 vintage, AAA tranches of sub prime CDO securities dropped from 100 to 70. Based on an 85% original loan to value assumption, a price of 70 would imply the entire pool of mortgages would go into default and the liquidation would realize on average less than 50% of the original price of the home. By early 2008, these AAA rated tranches were trading in the low 50 price range. This implies that the entire pool liquidates and the average foreclosure sale realizes less than 40% of its original sale price. This is full credit crunch fear mode.

Where are we now? By the last week of March 2008, banks had written off more than $318 billion in credit exposure and raised $225 billion in new capital. According to JP Morgan CIO Michael Cembalest, in a recent "Eye on the Market" report, this is not the "worst credit crisis ever." As one of those who saw the storm coming, Cembalest certainly deserves respect for his relatively calm analysis of where we are today. Looking at the existence of 30-to-1 leveraged SIVs, and banks utterly immobilized by bad real estate loans, it's nevertheless remarkable to hear his conclusion which states, "normalized for all these things, spreads and prices are more or less right where you would expect them to be."[5]

The credit crisis atmosphere peaked in March 2008 and forced Bear Stearns to sell its remaining assets to JP Morgan, over a weekend, for 2% of what the firm had been worth the previous summer. The fear of leverage and the uncertainty of the value of what was on the company's books made the usual financing markets unwilling to lend to Bear Stearns, forcing them to sell their company. By April 2008, however, the worst was past. Credit spreads were still elevated, but they had narrowed from the crisis levels of the previous month. Federal Reserve Bank intervention to support the interbank market worked to calm nervousness and return market flows to more normal levels.

Assessment

The key to price in the housing market is supply and demand. Commerce Department figures indicate that new home construction proceeded at a little over 2 million units per year between 2004 and 2006.[6] At the current rate of about 1 million new home starts per year, it will take roughly three years to work off the excess inventory. There may be a fairly long period of soft housing prices, but that doesn't necessarily mean that the market will go much lower.

Based on the National Association of Realtors Housing Affordability Index which compares median family household income to the cost of buying a used home, the typical family had 129% of the income required to buy a home in the year 2000 (assuming a 20% down payment), but by June 2007 the typical family only had 104.9% of the required income.[7] Median family household income had increased from $50,000 to $59,000 over the same period; however, home prices had risen at a much faster pace. As of March 2008, the index had improved to 130.2, primarily through the drop in home prices, which is back in the range of affordability seen during the years from 1995 to 2000, when the housing boom started.

By any reasonable assessment, the housing crisis is about over. Prices may remain weak for another year or so, as inventories are reduced, but housing is more affordable today than it was one year ago. Based on the affordability index, housing is within 10% of its most affordable level in 20 years. Americans want to own their homes, and the aftermath of the sub prime crisis should be a period when cheaper homes are available to those who can afford the down payments and have the credit standing to buy them.

The pain for the banks, the builders, and those who were over extended will turn out to be a long-term boon to homebuyers in this country as they scoop up affordable homes. The good news becomes, this is a good time to buy a home. The choice is wide, prices can be negotiated, and buying a home has rarely been more affordable than it is now. We may not have reached the bottom of the market just yet, but it is nevertheless a long-term opportunity for those with the ability and the confidence to buy themselves a home at a great price.

16

Health Care Reality

CONVENTIONAL WISDOM

Millions of Americans have no health care and no way to get it, because they can't afford it.

Typical Headlines

"Health Insurance 'Unaffordable'"
—*Las Vegas Review-Journal, Sept. 8, 2005*

"More Working Americans Go Without Health Care Coverage"
—*USA Today, May 5, 2006*

"47 Million Americans Are Uninsured:
11.7% Census Data Fuel Attacks by Democrats"
—*Boston Globe, Aug. 29, 2007*

Facts

For years, we've heard that upwards of 45 million Americans do not have health insurance, as if this statistic alone proves the need for nationalized health care. The problem with this piece of information is that the number is misleading and the implications are false. First, the statistic ignores the fact that 10 million of the uninsured are residents but not American citizens. Even with nationalized health insurance, most of these people would not be covered. Secondly, as reported recently in the *New York Times*, the totals cited by alarmists include more than 14 million Americans who are eligible for Medicaid but, for whatever reasons, have not enrolled. Medicaid is available to those who are unable to pay for their own medical care. And, finally, these figures also include large numbers of people who *can* afford to pay for their own medical care, and who *can* afford health insurance if they so desire, but don't want it.

Another claim we often hear is that "as many as 40 million people in this country do not have access to health care," which is also a false and misleading statement. Every American has access to health care of one kind or another, whether or not they have health insurance. The Public Health Service provides care for poor and indigent patients, including many illegal aliens. On average, each individual treated in the public health system receives $1,500 in free medical care per year, and as much as $6,000 per year for a family of four.[1]

The fact is, by federal law, no one can ever be denied treatment in an emergency room. While the cost, both to the hospital and the government, for this accommodation is excessive and generally unfair to those who ultimately pay the costs, it is nevertheless a fact of life. And the result of currently existing entitlement programs—including compassionate care in medical emergencies—is that the U.S. government pays for and controls more than half of all health care in this country, and the American taxpayer is already footing the bill.[2]

No country on earth spends more money per person on health care than the U.S. According to statistics published by the Cato Institute, health care consumers are annually spending more than $1.8 trillion for overall health costs, which is more than we spend on housing, food, national defense, or automobiles.[3] And according to one recent report, the government pays directly or indirectly for more than half of the nation's health care. Third party payment systems, however, actually come from a wide variety of private insurers, for-profit hospitals, and employers who often add cost without adding any individual incentive to question or control cost.

Assessment

The U.S. spends more on health care per capita, and spends a larger percentage of its GDP on health care and medical systems, than any other industrialized nation. In effect, more than 85% of Americans have health insurance of some kind, and 100% of Americans have access to basic medical care, whether or not they can afford to pay.

Many who complain about the current system don't realize that the government (i.e., taxpayers) is already paying over half of all health care costs, which is a dramatic change from forty years ago when the government only paid about 10% of health-care costs. Yet those who argue that the high cost of health care somehow justifies nationalized health care and total government control often don't recognize how much of that high cost is due to current government programs, medical providers high insurance costs and federally mandated regulations.

Facts

According to the Bureau of Labor Statistics, health care is the largest industry in America, providing 13.6 million jobs for wage and salaried workers, and about 438,000 jobs for the self-employed. Seven of the 20 fastest growing occupations in America today are health-care related, and it's projected that between now and the year 2016, the industry will generate more than 3 million new jobs—more than any other industry.

Physicians and diagnostic practitioners are among the country's best educated workers; however, most of the workers in hospitals and health-care facilities occupy positions that require less than a four-year

TOTAL HEALTH EXPENDITURES PER CAPITA, U.S. AND SELECTED COUNTRIES, 2003

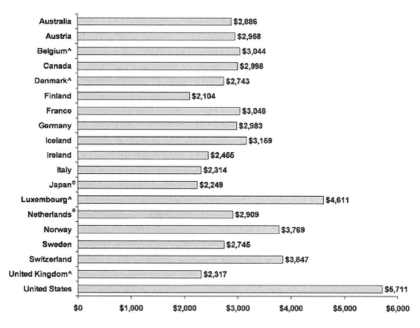

Source: Organisation for Economic Co-operation and Development. OECD Health Data 2006, from OECD Internet subscription database updated October 10, 2006. Copyright OECD 2006. Available at: http://www.oecd.org/health/healthdata

Note: Amount in U.S. Dollars PPP[4]

* OECD estimate.

college education. That's a lot of involvement, and a lot of brainpower dedicated to maintaining and improving the system.

Another way to see the level of public involvement in this industry is to look at how much of a country's national income is spent on health care. The chart below, prepared by analysts of the Kaiser Family Foundation, shows that in 2003 health expenditures in this country came to 15.2% of U.S. GDP—at least three percentage points higher than for any other country in the analysis. Since the 1970s, the U.S.

has committed a higher share of GDP to health care than most other nations, although several other countries had comparable spending levels in 1970 and 1980.

Since that time, however, health-care spending as a share of GDP has grown more rapidly in the U.S. Between 1980 and 2003, the U.S. share of GDP devoted to health grew by 6.4%, which is more than 2% more than any other country analyzed in the Kaiser study. A separate report by Uwe Reinhardt of Princeton University estimates that health care costs may top 28% of U.S. GDP by the year 2030.

CONVENTIONAL WISDOM

Universal health care would solve all our problems and improve health care for most Americans.

Typical Headlines

"Growing Health Care Concerns Fuel Cautious Support for Change"
—*ABC News, Oct. 20, 2003*

"How Veterans' Hospitals Became the Best in Health Care"
—*Time, Aug. 27, 2006*

"Americans Want Universal Health Care"
—*USA Today, Sept. 25, 2006*

Facts

When it comes to health care, the old saying, "There's no such thing as a free lunch," is correct. In their assessment of the U.S. health-care dilemma published in the *Chicago Tribune*, Dr. Ezekiel J. Emanuel, who is chair of the department of bioethics at the Clinical Center of the National Institutes of Health, and Dr. Victor R. Fuchs, a professor

of economics at Stanford University, offered the following strong dose
of reality:

> Americans believe employers pay the bulk of workers' premi-
> ums, government pays for Medicare, Medicaid and the State
> Children's Health Insurance Program, and individuals pay some
> premiums as well as deductibles and co-pays. This is wrong.
> Business, government and individuals do not share the finan-
> cial responsibility for health coverage. Individuals bear the full
> cost of health care through lower wages and taxes.[5]

Unfortunately, a lot of Americans aren't getting the picture. An
ABC News/*Washington Post* poll conducted by telephone in October
2003, with a random sample of 1,000 adults, found that 62% of those
surveyed would prefer a national program of universal health care to the
current employee-based system in this country, while just under a third
said they preferred to leave things alone. However, respondents also
said that if a nationalized system would mean restrictions on patients'
choice of physicians or longer waiting lists for non-emergency treatment, fewer than 40% would favor the idea of universal health care.[6]

For the first time in the last twenty years, more than half of respondents to the ABC poll (54%) said they're dissatisfied with the quality
of health care in this country. However, it was also noted that 82% of
those with existing coverage have a positive view of the health care system. And among respondents who said they had experienced a serious
or chronic illness in their family during the previous year, 91% said
they were satisfied with the care they received, and 86% said they were
satisfied with their medical coverage.

Among all Americans, including those who lack health insurance,
large majorities expressed overall satisfaction with their quality of
health care (85%), with their ability to see a doctor (83%), their ability
to see a specialist (78%), and their ability to get the most sophisticated
treatment available (77%). With such high approval ratings for the

current system, one has to wonder what the 62% who said they favor universal health care can be thinking.

Among those without health insurance, ratings were generally lower; however, 69% of those respondents still rated the quality of their health care positively; 73% were positive about their ability to see a doctor; 55% were satisfied with their ability to see a top-quality specialist when needed; and 58% were satisfied with their ability to get the latest treatments.

Assessment

What the opinion polls actually show is the degree to which the public has been confused and divided by media coverage of this issue. Older Americans are naturally nervous about the availability and quality of health care and, in some cases, may be led to give unrepresentative answers to polls of this nature, in order to express their concern. Those few younger Americans who actually respond to polls of this type tend to report what they hear from friends, news reports, or the conventional wisdom of their peers.

A 2007 Harris/*Wall Street Journal* poll found that 76% of respondents thought that a nationalized health insurance plan for individuals who are uninsured under the current system was a good idea. However, when asked if they were willing to pay higher taxes to support the Medicare and Medicaid expenses of those individuals, the numbers flipped, with only 26% responding in the affirmative. In the abstract, most Americans think it would be a good idea to help the poor and disadvantaged; but when they understand the social and economic realities involved, most people tend to take a much more practical view.

A 2008 study from the Harvard School of Public Health reported that Americans are split by political party over whether they think socialized medicine would make the U.S. health-care system better or worse. In a survey conducted by university researchers, 70% of Republicans said national health care would be worse than the current system, while 70% of Democrats said it would be better.[7] Again, the issue isn't whether or not the existing system is satisfactory or if the quality of care is adequate, but other factors, such as economic feasibility, or belief in the government's ability to manage this massive and diverse industry.

Managing an Unruly Giant

A comprehensive study of the cost of government health-care regulation and the cost of medical care by Christopher Conover, a research professor at Duke University, reveals that the total cost of health services regulation in this country exceeds $339.2 billion. That figure includes regulation of health facilities, health professionals, health insurance, drugs and medical devices, and the medical tort system, including the costs of "defensive medicine."

Even if the analysts were to subtract the $170 billion in savings provided by certain beneficial regulatory measures, the net cost of health-care regulation still tops $169 billion annually. In other words, as the report's author concludes, the costs of health services regulation outweighs the benefits by a factor of two-to-one, and government's involvement in overseeing existing systems costs the average household more than $1,500 per year.[8]

But the darkest chapter of this story isn't necessarily the skyrocketing financial costs, but the costs in terms of human dignity and well-being. In the U.K., Canada, Scandinavia, and other places where national health care has been implemented, it can take from four to six months simply to get an appointment to see a physician. At that point, it may take more weeks and months to be admitted for treatment, even when the treatment is for serious illnesses, including heart disease, cancer, or other potentially fatal conditions.

Since costs and access to treatment in these national programs are rationed by government regulators, elderly patients often find themselves at a distinct disadvantage, and may be denied care altogether. Younger patients with longer life expectancy are generally given first priority in these systems. And because everything from the price of medicine to the salaries paid to doctors and nurses are regulated by the government, patients can suffer because of cost-cutting measures that hold down costs but penalize the individual patient.

In June 2001, a study of patient care under Britain's National Health Service (NHS) showed that more than 1,038,000 citizens of that country were on the hospital waiting lists, with no guarantee they would ever see a physician. Of those, 76,000 had been on the list for more than three months. Some had been waiting for as long as eighteen months, and many of these had long-term and potentially fatal diseases.

But the citizens of Britain and Canada aren't the only ones complaining. Other studies report that thousands of British and Canadian doctors are emigrating to this country because of their government's limitations on what they can and cannot prescribe for their patients. Physicians' requests for treatment authorization for serious health issues are frequently, and inexplicably, refused by the bureaucracy. In some cases this is reportedly due to cost controls; in other cases it appears to be the whim of the particular bureaucrat who fields the request.

A Bureaucratic Nightmare

The left-wing filmmaker Michael Moore boasted in his mockumentary, "Sicko," that the national health services of Britain, Canada, and even Cuba, were far superior to the American system. But, in fact, large numbers of Britons and Canadians are forced to go abroad to get the treatment they need, traveling to other parts of Europe, Asia, and even farther away for better and faster access to medical care. Needless to say, Cubans aren't free to travel anywhere.

Most of the European and Canadian "health tourists" wind up paying for treatment out of their own pockets, despite the fact that most are already paying as much as 20% in taxes in their home country for "free health care." According to a report in the *London Sunday*

Telegraph, more than 70,000 Britons traveled abroad for medical treatment in 2007 alone. And the NHS estimates that as many as 200,000 Britons will choose to leave the U.K. for treatment by the end of this decade.[9]

Patients are reportedly traveling to Germany, Poland, Spain, Hungary, and Turkey, and some even travel as far as India, Pakistan, and Malaysia for treatment. The Internet website TreatmentAbroad.com reports that Britons have traveled to 112 foreign hospitals in 48 countries to find safe, affordable care. Because of crowding, inattentive health-care providers, and other lax conditions in many of Britain's public hospitals and clinics, there has recently been a chilling rise in serious infections from the spread of *Staphylococcus* bacteria and other viral illnesses in unsanitary conditions.

The *Telegraph* article indicates that there has been a 500-percent increase in diagnosed cases of the deadly superbug *Clostridium difficile* in just the last 10 years. No wonder a spokesperson for Britain's Patients' Association told reporters that, "People are simply frightened of going to NHS hospitals, so I am not surprised the numbers going abroad are increasing so rapidly." The emotional stress and expense of escaping from the NHS can be extreme, and those who go are often forced into difficult financial straits as a result. But a nationwide survey reported that almost all those who have traveled abroad for treatment say they would gladly do it again if the need should arise.

What About the Clinton Plan?

The main components of the nationalized health plan first promoted by Senator Hillary Clinton in 1993, and modified slightly in her 2008 presidential campaign, is essentially a federally mandated insurance program. What the candidate has called the "American Health Choices Plan" is an "individual mandate" that would require all Americans to purchase health insurance, with the guarantee that the government will make insurance available to everyone at "affordable prices." To accomplish this, her plan would create a government-regulated national pool from which individuals would be able to purchase the insurance they need. Those already insured under existing programs would be able to choose whether or not to keep their current health coverage or switch to the national plan. But health insurance would no longer be optional.

The Clinton plan would also force businesses that don't offer health insurance to pay a new "Health Choices Tax." In order for a health insurance provider to sell their policy in the national pool, the federal government would demand that insurers cover all applicants, regardless of pre-existing health conditions or ability to pay, and that premium levels would be indiscriminate, regardless of the individual's health status when they apply. All premiums would be determined by the government and wouldn't be allowed to exceed a predetermined percentage of the insured's total household income. Senator Clinton's advisers have said the plan will cost U.S. taxpayers an additional $110 billion per year.[10] But if biased proponents of the plan admit to an annual cost of $110 billion, we can only wonder what the actual cost would turn out to be.

The Senator says her program would provide universal coverage for all Americans, but this also means that the program will be mandatory and will impose a universal tax to pay for it. Still, there's no guarantee the quality of care provided by the plan would be comparable to the care currently available in the free market system. Most of those who are currently uninsured are individuals who are not willing to pay for insurance, whether private or public. Some may be healthy enough not to feel the need for health insurance. Others may simply want to avoid another large monthly expense. A sign of the lack of enthusiasm for such programs is the fact that only about half of those qualified for coverage under the State Child Health Insurance Program (SCHIP) have bothered to enroll.

Before we suddenly decide that government ought to be paying more for our health care, we need to pause long enough to see who's really paying these costs. The health-care specialists cited above make the point very well in their *Chicago Tribune* article, where they write:

> The government's funds for health care don't come from governors, senators, representatives or the president. When government pays for increases in health-care costs, it taxes current citizens, borrows—asking future taxpayers to foot the bill—or reduces other state services that benefit citizens. Health-care costs are now the single largest state expenditure, exceeding even education.[11]

Whenever "government" is asked to pay for anything, they simply increase your taxes. And the bigger the program, the more you will pay.

CONVENTIONAL WISDOM

The private Health Savings Accounts (HSA) promoted by the Bush administration would not be adequate to handle the medical needs of most Americans.

Typical Headlines

"The Health-Care IRA. Are you ready?"
    —*CNNMoney.com, Sept. 22, 2004*

"Bush Promotes Health Savings Accounts"
    —*Washington Post, Jan. 27, 2005*

"Health Savings Accounts: A Bad Idea Whose Time Has Come?"
    —*Mother Jones, Jan. 26, 2006*

Facts

One of the major benefits of the Health Savings Accounts (HSA) proposed by the Bush administration is that these tax-protected accounts will allow consumers to avoid higher taxes and, at the same time, escape the rising costs of health care. Because they offer lower premiums and a high-deductible approach, HSAs will make health insurance more affordable for most Americans. An indication of how dollar-smart they are is the fact that many banks, insurance companies, and mutual funds have switched to HSAs for their employees. Many financial analysts are now saying that HSAs are superior to the Roth IRAs, which have served a similar purpose in the past.[12]

It's true that the federal government is picking up more of the tab for America's medical bills. Studies by the Centers for Medicare and Medicaid Services report that total spending on personal health is expected to double over the next eight years to more than $4 trillion. At that point, they say, government programs such as Medicare, Medicaid, and SCHIP will account for about half of all health spending, and taxpayers will be less free to choose private health insurance for their families.

Assessment

Ever since proposals for universal health care first began making headlines in this country in the early-1990s, university researchers, sociologists, and pundits in some of America's liberal think tanks have been at the forefront of the debate, offering ideas, proposals, and theories to support the prospect of universal health care. Recently, however, as pointed out in a new study from the National Bureau of Economic Research (NBER) at Harvard University, some of these public figures seem to have changed their minds and decided that socialized medicine doesn't actually work. In a survey of academics in 20 developed countries, the NBER survey found the following surprising conclusions:

1. There is no general relationship between the way countries pay for health care and their ability to control costs. Public versus private financing, general revenue versus payroll taxes, third-party versus out-of-pocket spending—nothing seems to matter very much.

2. Government provision of health care is only modestly progres-
    sive. In Canada, people in the bottom two income quintiles—
    which represents 40% of the population—receive about 50%
    of all the health care benefits. Moreover, relative to health
    care needs, Canada's health care spending may not be pro-
    gressive at all. That is, the benefits of the subsidized programs
    may not be going to those at the lower end of the economic
    spectrum. Among people with similar health conditions in the
    European Community, "higher income people use the system
    more intensively and use more costly services than do lower
    income people."

3. Marginal increases in health care spending may actually be
    regressive, meaning that the benefits of the program may be
    serving those who are least in need of government assistance,
    while those with the greatest need often go unserved. This is
    especially true if extra spending buys specialist services and
    elective procedures. "In Canada, high income people make dis-
    proportionate use of elective surgical procedures, such as hip
    and knee replacements."

4. Most surprising perhaps, the academics concluded that govern-
    ment provision of health care has little impact on the general
    well-being of society. When economists assign a dollar value to
    health care and add it to monetary income, national health
    insurance has very little impact on overall economic inequality.
    Providing universal health care does not elevate the status of
    the poor, and does not heal all of society's wounds, as some had
    expected.

5. On the other hand, increases in health care spending crowd out
    other government programs. Redistribution through govern-
    ment-funded health care partly replaces other redistributive gov-
    ernment programs, the report says, and penalizes the broader
    spectrum of government-funded initiatives. What low-income
    people gain in health services may be offset by reductions in
    housing or education benefits. Which means that, in the end,

there is no good reason to change what we're doing now, particularly since the American health care industry is universally recognized as one of the best, if not "the best," in the world.[13]

Toward a Real World Solution

Unfortunately, health care is never a "one size fits all" affair. The needs of adults and children can vary greatly, and the variance in the treatments prescribed for accident victims, the chronically or terminally ill, and those who opt for elective surgery are as different as night and day. There are significant differences in treatments for men and women, as well, and under today's system of private care and personal health insurance, individuals are free to opt for clinics and board-certified physicians who specialize in the areas of medicine that are most helpful to their needs. By its very nature, however, this is not an environment in which government customarily succeeds.

Catastrophic health insurance can be a god-send for those who find themselves incapacitated by strokes, cancers, heart disease, or other debilitating conditions. But, again, this is not an area where government-funded health insurance is likely to be of much help. When the state is paying for it, there's no guarantee of a high level of personal care. It's in the best interest of physicians and other health-care providers to please their clients, and in a government-funded system where Uncle Sam is paying the bills, that means the well-being of the patient may not be the health care provider's first priority.

According to an insightful commentary in the *Wall Street Journal*, the most important change government can make to improve health care in America would be to reduce the amount of regulation on health care providers, insurers, and the medical service industry. As previously stated, the real culprit in this whole business is the high cost of medical care imposed by federal regulations. As the *Journal* article points out, "Each percentage-point rise in health-insurance costs increases the number of uninsured by 300,000 people."[14] In other words, the escalating cost of the annual insurance premium will drive large numbers of Americans out of the market.

This, in turn, creates a vicious spiral, because when healthy individuals opt out of insurance, the costs for those who remain in the program will naturally rise. For many employees, the rising cost of health insurance can be a serious drain on disposable income, and this is one of the major reasons for the large numbers of uninsured so often cited by the media.

The long and short of it is that the answer to America's health care problem is not more regulation, more taxes, and more federal control. A free-market system is the best way to rein in costs, to encourage innovation in treatment and care, and to improve quality overall. The first step in fixing the system ought to be recognizing that current federal regulations and policies mandated by Congress are preventing the market from doing its job. If Congress would spend as much time simplifying the bizarre network of rules and regulations that restrict free enterprise as they do erecting hurdles for the health care industry to leap over, things would get better before you know it.

Poorly conceived federal tax policies, insurance regulations, and barriers to participation in the system have taken the decision-making away from the consumer and put it into the hands of third-party payers, which has devastated competition and led directly to today's health-care crisis.

A Critical Assessment

The key to reducing the U.S. health-care system's excessive cost without damaging its ability to innovate is to allow competitive market forces to operate. These forces have worked in every other market to keep costs low and improve quality. There is no reason why they won't work in health care. Attacking the tax code's bias against efficient and cost-effective health insurance is fundamental to creating an economically sound health-care system.

—*John F. Cogan*[15]

We can only concur with the authors cited above when they say that America's health-care policy has arrived at a dangerous crossroads. What we decide in the coming months will make a huge difference in how well we live, and how dependable our health-care options will be for the foreseeable future. Either we will continue on the march toward a government-regulated nightmare of a health-care system, or we will decide at long last that a free-market solution that puts consumers back in charge of their own destiny is the only reasonable option.

The federally-controlled policies and promises being made by politicians in Washington can only lead to fewer choices and a serious lack of innovation. A free-market solution, on the other hand, will put the future of our health-care system back into the hands of consumers and their doctors, where it belongs.

17

Nifty NAFTA

CONVENTIONAL WISDOM

The North American Free Trade Alliance (NAFTA) has allowed Mexico and Canada to flood this country with substandard goods and drive down U.S. wages.

Typical Headlines

"Mexico: Was NAFTA Worth It?"
—*BusinessWeek, Dec. 22, 2003*

"Lost Jobs Blamed on Trade Accord"
—*Seattle Times, Sept. 29, 2006*

"Exploring Reasons Why NAFTA Has Been Bad for U.S."
—*Louisville Courier-Journal, Apr. 14, 2008*

Facts

Since the NAFTA trade and tariff agreements went into effect on January 1, 1994, replacing the U.S.–Canada Free Trade Agreement implemented in 1989, real hourly compensation in the U.S. business sector has risen by 1.5% each year, for a total of 23.6% over the last fourteen years. By comparison, in the fourteen years from 1979 to 1993, the annual rate of real hourly compensation increased just 0.7% each year, or 11% overall.

Rather than hurting jobs in this country, NAFTA has, in fact, boosted the rate of new job creation. Between December 1993 and December 2006, U.S. employment rose from 112.2 million to 137.2 million jobs, a 22% increase, with a total of 25 million new jobs. On the other hand, the average rate of unemployment during the same period was 5.1%, compared to 7.1% during the period 1981–1993.

In addition, NAFTA has boosted manufacturing as well, with output increasing by 63% between 1993 and 2006, topping the 37% increase in manufacturing between 1980 and 1993.[1] And wages for manufacturing workers have gone up. Average real compensation grew at an average annual rate of 1.6% from 1993 to 2006, compared to 0.9% between 1980 and 1993.

CONVENTIONAL WISDOM

Lowering tariffs and throwing open the borders to U.S. markets for Canada and Mexico will hurt business in this country.

Typical Headlines

"Sour Taste of NAFTA: Old Friends Become Foes"
        —*New York Times, Nov. 7, 1997*

"NAFTA: An Unreliable Ally"
        —*The Economist, Mar. 6, 2008*

"Pennsylvania Stagnation: Is NAFTA the Culprit?"
        —*New York Times, Apr. 15, 2008*

Facts

Again, since NAFTA went into effect, both trade and investment have increased substantially in this country and across the borders with Mexico and Canada. From 1993 to 2006, trade among the three NAFTA partners has climbed 198%, from $297 billion to $883 billion. Exports of U.S. goods to those countries grew even faster. While exports to all other countries grew at a rate of 108%, trade with Mexico and Canada grew at a rate of 157%. The net result is that business has boomed since the NAFTA accords were put in place.

NAFTA partners, Canada and Mexico, purchased $18.2 million worth of agricultural products, which accounted for 29.6% of total U.S. agricultural exports in 2004 alone, up from 20.8% in 1993.

Boosting North-American Investment

According to the most recent U.S. Department of Agriculture (USDA) figures, Mexico and Canada have become two of the top three U.S.

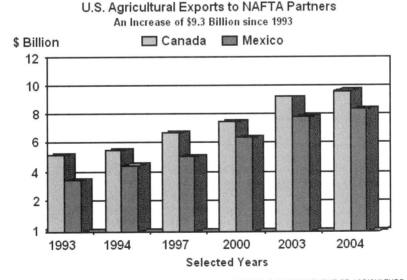

U.S. Agricultural Exports to NAFTA Partners
An Increase of $9.3 Billion since 1993

SOURCE: U.S. DEPARTMENT OF AGRICULTURE.

poultry markets in the world. In 2004, U.S. poultry exports to Mexico were valued at $331.1 million, while Canada reached $330.3 million (the Russian Federation came in at $530.5 million). Exports to Mexico increased 61.5%, and increased 100% to Canada since 1993. Export increases from 2003 are especially remarkable, at 27.6% for Mexico and 22.8% for Canada.

At the same time, U.S. pork producers credit NAFTA with their gains in market share in Mexico for pork products, which increased 3.5 times to $430.7 million between 1993 and 2004, and more than seven-fold to $259.8 million to Canada during the same period. One-year increases from 2003 to 2004 are striking, as well, as exports to Mexico and Canada surged 93.6% and 49% respectively.

Exports of U.S. fresh fruits and vegetables to Canada, our top market, reached $1.9 billion in 2004. This is an increase of 45.5% since 1993, and 5% since 2003. Mexico's growth as a market for these products is even more impressive, according to the USDA, rising from America's fifth largest market in 1993 to the third largest in 2004. Exports to Mexico surged 98%, from $134 million in 1993 to $265.8 million in 2004. Changes between 2003 and 2004 were mixed, as exports to Canada rose 5% while exports to Mexico declined by 0.5%.[2]

In addition, investment in business, which is important for maintaining a high standard of living in the NAFTA countries, has increased substantially. Excluding housing, U.S. non-residential business investment has increased by 107% since 1993, compared to 45% between 1980 and 1993. The result is that U.S. economic growth over this same period has been remarkably strong, and the cooperation between these North American partners continues to bring opportunities for new growth opportunities.

The trade deficit with Canada for U.S. goods was $72.8 billion in 2006, a decrease of $5.7 billion from the $78.5 billion reported in 2005. In 2006, U.S. exports totaled $230.6 billion, up 8.8% from the previous year. During this time, U.S. imports from Canada were $303.4 billion, up 4.5%. Canada is currently the largest export market for U.S. goods.

U.S. exports of private commercial services to Canada, excluding military and government-related trade, were $32.5 billion in 2005 (latest data available), and U.S. imports were $22.0 billion. Sales of services in Canada by majority U.S.-owned affiliates were $46.9 billion in 2004 (latest data available), while sales of services in the United States by majority Canada-owned firms were $36.6 billion. Meanwhile, the stock of U.S. Foreign Direct Investment (FDI) in Canada in 2005 was $234.8 billion, up from $212.8 billion in 2004. U.S. FDI activity in Canada is concentrated primarily in the manufacturing, finance, and mining sectors.

CONVENTIONAL WISDOM

Reducing tariffs and trade barriers, giving both Mexico and Canada unlimited access to the U.S. marketplace, will escalate the trade deficit and further penalize American business.

Typical Headlines

"Treaty Called 'Job Killer'"
—*Raleigh-Durham New & Observer, May 11, 2005*

"NAFTA's Seven-Year Itch: Trade Deficits Explode"
—*Economic Policy Institute, Sept. 28, 2006*

"Hold NAFTA Accountable: Withdraw If It Doesn't Work"
—*The Hill, Dec. 7, 2007*

Facts

The primary fear, repeated in many political venues and by many in the mainstream media, is that NAFTA destroys jobs. That fear is neatly encapsulated by the following statement from the Public Citizen website:

Here are the more relevant numbers: U.S. manufacturing employment declined from 16.8 million people in 1993 to

13.9 million people in 2007, a decrease of nearly 3 million manufacturing jobs, and nearly 20% of the total. Moreover, the $190 billion U.S. trade deficit with NAFTA countries—as a simple accounting matter—corresponds to manufacturing jobs that could have been here. The Economic Policy Institute estimates that the United States could have had over one million additional manufacturing jobs had there been trade balance between NAFTA countries alone. This figure subtracts from the NAFTA trade deficit our oil and gas trade deficit, which has always been significant, although it has shrunk 40% as a share of our total deficit since the deal went into effect.[3]

It's hard to believe that all job losses in the U.S. manufacturing sector are related to NAFTA, since the U.S. goods deficit with its NAFTA partners, excluding oil import/export, is about $45 billion annually, or about 0.3% of GDP. Trade with NAFTA is huge and valuable allowing the US to focus on what it does best and allowing our partners to do the same. The net of the buys and sells is just 0.3% of GDP. Even if you believe that 0.3% of GDP has that much impact on jobs and wages, there are other larger trends to be considered. Total industrial production jobs peaked at around 25 million in 1974, long before NAFTA. Since then, production jobs, which include manufacturing, have trended down to near 20 million.

At the same time, as industrial production jobs have dropped about 5 million total, U.S. industrial output since 1974 has more than doubled. Clearly U.S. industrial output and employment has primarily been responding to productivity changes. The clearest way of tracking NAFTA related job losses is the number of claims filed under the Trade Adjustment Assistance Act. Since 1994, 1.8 million claims have been accepted for reimbursement under this act, which covers many areas, including manufacturing.

There are limitations to this number, since not all claims are accepted, and it's not simple to qualify. However, even if you assume the correct number is not 1.8 million but triple that (or 5.4 million), that is still only 105,000 jobs per quarter over 13 years. The government's JOLTS Survey, which reports on job losses and gains, indicates that the U.S. creates and eliminates millions of jobs each quarter. An extra 105,000 job, plus or minus, is not likely to create a major shift in overall employment patterns.

Since the 1970s, as industrial jobs have dropped, the average unemployment rate has also dropped. In the 1970s, 6% was considered full employment, but since 1992 the U.S. unemployment rate has averaged 5.2%. The broad indicators clearly do not support the argument that the job market as a whole has been hurt by NAFTA, even if some areas and some jobs have been lost.

An Accurate Picture

If you believe everything the political candidates are saying, you would have to believe that NAFTA is responsible for the loss of some 3 mil-

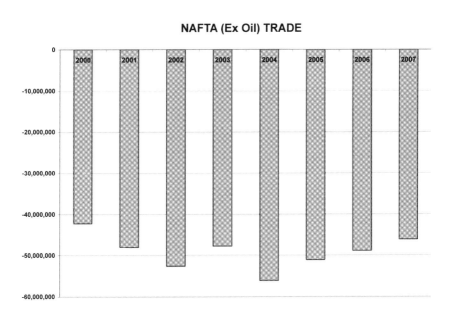

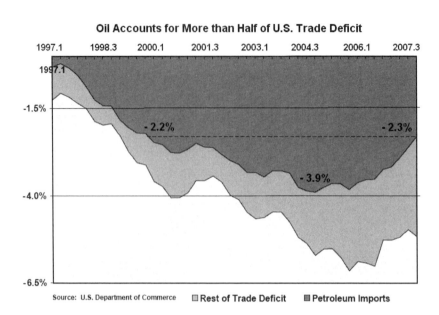

Oil Accounts for More than Half of U.S. Trade Deficit

Source: U.S. Department of Commerce   ☐ Rest of Trade Deficit   ■ Petroleum Imports

lion jobs in the manufacturing sector, or that outsourcing production to Mexico and Canada has led to an "exploding trade deficit." Unfortunately, such claims may be long on drama, but they're short on facts. An insightful commentary in the *Wall Street Journal* by former Michigan Governor John Engler points out that the trade imbalance has nothing to do with NAFTA, but instead is primarily due to the high volume of oil imports.

As discussed in Chapter 10, Canada and Mexico are the number-one and number-two suppliers of crude oil to the United States. In September 2007, the U.S. imported more than 75 billion barrels of oil from Canada, which was 18.3% of total oil imports. At the same time, we imported 43.6 billion barrels from Mexico, for 10.65% of the total. More recently, in January 2008, the U.S. imported 71.4 billion barrels from Canada, or 19.5% of the total, and 38.5 billion barrels from Mexico, which was 10.5% of all crude oil imports.

Petroleum imports accounted for 55% of the entire U.S. trade deficit in the fourth quarter of 2007. Outside of oil and gas imports, the U.S.

U.S. Imports of Crude Oil by Selected Countries, 2005
(Quantity and Customs Value)

Country	Quantity (Thousand barrels)	Customs Value ($million)
Total World	3,753,088	175,563
OPEC Total	1,818,357	88,303
Saudi Arabia	524,129	24,739
Venezuela	535,718	24,074
Nigeria	396,918	21,904
Kuwait	80,396	3,702
Algeria	82,383	4,670
Other OPEC	198,813	9,214
Non-OPEC Total	1,934,732	87,260
Canada	567,676	24,148
Mexico	552,076	23,096
Angola	161,507	8,161
Ecuador	99,128	4,223
Norway	43,107	1,947
Gabon	55,792	2,759
Other Non-OPEC	455,446	22,926

Source: U.S. Census Bureau, *U.S. International Trade in Goods and Services*, FT-900, issued monthly.

trade deficit has narrowed by 40% over the past three years and now, at 2.3% of GDP, is at the lowest level since 1999. As Gov. Engler points out, the trade deficit has almost doubled between 2000 and 2007, from $77 billion at the turn of the century to $140 billion in 2007. Nevertheless, the problem was not in manufactured goods but in energy imports. Of the $62 billion increase in trade deficits since NAFTA began, $58 billion (95% of the total) is energy related. Except for energy, the trade deficit with our NAFTA partners has grown by just $3.5 billion since 2000, less than 0.03% of GDP while sales of agricultural and manufactured goods to Canada and Mexico have almost kept pace with imports.

If U.S. trade with the rest of the world performed at the same levels as with NAFTA countries, the U.S. non-energy trade deficit would only have grown by $25 billion, instead of the actual growth of $155 billion.

18

Wake up America

We are both the most imitated and hated culture in the world. We have both the most trusted and the most feared military power. We are the world's largest maker of things, seller of goods and buyer of the world's products. What we do matters and we can't afford to make decisions that will affect the future merely based on what we want to believe is true. We need to look beyond headlines and investigate the world as it is to make good choices based on an understanding of our nation's many strengths and actual needs.

People love to see whatever or whoever is on top brought down. This yearning is part of the human condition and it is why recent stories about Britney, Paris, and failed high profile executives attracted lots of eyeballs. The desire to see the mighty fall explains some of the recent Bush bashing and Clinton bashing before it, as well as the hatred toward America over the past half century. But during the past five years this inclination, spurred by the combination of media bias, partisan anger over contentious presidential elections, and a highly controversial war in Iraq, evolved into a palpable hatred and led to much of the irresponsible media narrative.

Unfortunately Bush bashing coalesced with America bashing, even among some Americans, and as a result falsehoods that were emotionally gratifying became accepted conventional wisdom. Be careful. The jokes were funny and the bashing may have filled a need, but the resulting misconceptions could be dangerous if they serve as the basis for misguided decisions.

America is far from perfect, and the constant striving to make it better should never stop, but finding a few imperfections doesn't mean the whole thing is a disaster. The truth is, our system is still a shining example to the world of what can be accomplished when the principles of free trade, democracy, and the rule of law are respected and applied. To make this point anything less than crystal clear does a disservice to those in emerging economies that so desperately need clear direction on how to fix their problems. And it's a disservice to the people of this country as well. Despite its imperfections, America remains the envy of the world. We need to appreciate what we have and fight for it or risk losing it.

The introduction of this book highlighted the difference between the liberal attitude of the press and the significantly less liberal view of the average American. There is no secret liberal cabal out to lie to America. But there is a view of the world, held in common among many of those who have chosen journalism as a profession that defines their narrative. Their choices of which stories will be highlighted and issues will be debated make sense to them based on what they consider important or what they believe will sell to the audience they have chosen.

In the 1950s, the common world view was the fear of communism and nuclear warfare. In a banal way that resulted in schoolchildren being trained to hide under their desks to prepare for a Nuclear attack. A more meaningful and sad outcome was McCarthyism, blacklists and arrests of anybody with a communist history. It all was driven by a narrative of a worldwide communist agenda that wanted to destroy America. McCarthy was popular; he was doing the people's work. Communism was a real threat but the response became irrational and destructive of American liberty.

Today we have different media narratives. Instead of the communist paranoia we are subjected to paranoia related to global warming, peak oil and the presumed utopia of universal health care. Oil, health care and pollution are important issues but what we hear about them is repetitive and narrow and is therefore not helpful in developing real alternatives and solutions. Since the media is not doing the job of providing an objective overview each individual must work harder to find useful information.

This book is designed to be helpful on some issues where obvious misconceptions exist, but we must all do our homework on the many key issues of our day. Due to the historical strength of our free market system of capitalism, Americans earn more than 20 times the average Asian worker and as a result American consumers are privileged to buy enormous quantities of wonderful things made in less developed countries that America couldn't begin to afford if they were built at American wage rates. So the U.S. gets all these goods and also employs its citizen to do more interesting, higher-value activities for work, and it all happens, with a trade deficit that, were it not for oil imports, is not unreasonable and would be declining rapidly.

More Americans own homes than ever and while home values are down 12% from the peak, they are still up 70% from 2001. The narrative in the media is only about the current fall in prices not the long term rise and gains to the homeowners.

The American citizen has the benefit of the best health care services in the world. The majority, 85% of the population have affordable health insurance. Those without insurance are guaranteed access to emergency rooms. No one is left out. This is not part of the media narrative. The American capitalistic system provides robust opportunities to move up (or down) an income ladder that offers unprecedented rewards to those who move up. It is not an easy system but it creates America's resilience and adaptability.

Seeing the Pattern: America Is Not "Broken"

We can not cover every important issue in this book, but we've tried to demonstrate a pattern. There is a huge perception/reality gap across many important issues. People have been told and seem to believe things are much worse than they really are. In other cases they have been told things are bad that are really good. This could lead to fixing problems that don't exist, which usually leads to real problems.

The American economy has not been a disaster. We reviewed the countries strengths in the first few chapters. In fact, America's real growth rate over the past six years ranks highly among developed nations, even though it is building on a stronger base. China is not about to usurp America for the global economic lead. In fact, the growth of the U.S. economy since President Bush took office—just the *increase*—is about equal to the *entire* economy of China. Tax cuts and military spending have not led to unprecedented budget deficits. In fact, the deficit is lower as a percent of Gross Domestic Product (GDP) than it was during the 70s, 80s, and 90s.

The wars in Iraq and Afghanistan are not bankrupting the U.S. In fact, defense spending has been lower, as a percent of GDP, during these wars than it was a dozen years earlier.

Social Security and Medicare are not just fine. In fact, the status quo is not sustainable. The narrative in the press seems to swing from positive to negative in line with Democratic Party talking points. Like all problems America has the strengths and tools to solve these problems, but first the country must face them factually and realistically. Hopefully you will find more resources to examine these problems.

"Tax cuts for the rich" have not led to a huge increase in income disparity. In fact, the top income earners are paying a higher percentage of taxes today than ever before. And income distribution has not changed significantly since 2000. The U.S. is not declining in global economic importance. After declining from as high as about 75% of World GDP in the mid-1940s to 21.7% in 1995, it increased to 27.5% in 2006.

The war in Afghanistan is not a failure. In fact, it has been an inspiring success story. More than 31 million Afghans have been freed from an oppressive theocracy, and al-Qaeda has been evicted, with a remarkably small loss of life.

The U.S. did not invade Iraq because Bush claimed with false certainty that Iraq had WMD, a fact that is lost in the current media narrative. The first reason given for invasion was *lack* of knowledge about Iraq's WMD. The U.S. invaded Iraq because Saddam Hussein did not comply with the treaty signed at the end of the First Gulf War and a dozen unanimously passed U.N. resolutions. The war in Iraq is not a failure. In fact, because of the hard work and sacrifices of our forces, Iraq is a tremendous success story. More than 28 million Iraqis were freed from a regime that enslaved, humiliated millions and killed hundreds of thousands of its own citizens. If we were to leave Iraq in an unstable condition, the long term impact on global stability could be dire. America has created two nascent multi-ethnic democracies in the Middle East. If they remain stable, successful and growing, think of the positive example for change that will provide the people of Syria and Iran.

Hurricane Katrina did not expose the incompetence and apathy of FEMA. In fact, the deployment of emergency provisions and personnel—before, during, and after the disaster—was the most extensive in the history of the United States. The misinformation in the media actually held back relief agencies and delayed the Red Cross and other volunteer organizations from sending in workers.

The Bush administration hasn't had a "failed, go-it-alone" foreign policy. In fact, the U.S.-led coalition in Iraq consisted of almost double the number of countries in the First Gulf War, and the coalition in Afghanistan includes an astonishing 82 countries. Of the five nations that posed a nuclear threat during George Bush's presidency, three have been eliminated (Iraq, Libya, and Syria), and another (North Korea) appears to be on the verge of being eliminated.[i] These are not the front page story of the media but the reality of these achievements should be a part of America's assessment of how to move forward and where to make changes.

Be Careful What you Wish For

Falling for convenient platitudes and making unwise or irresponsible changes could cost this nation more than America should be willing to pay. If the changes were large enough, the country could even lose the dynamic society which has created a land of opportunity and prosperity that has shown the way to so many people around the world for so many years.

The recent world food shortage is a perfect example of what can happen when decisions are made on the basis of emotions and wishful thinking defined by a commonly accepted view of the world instead of considering all the facts. The shortage was caused in part by the diversion of a significant amount of domestic corn and other vegetable products to the production of ethanol. Shortages of corn, rice, soybeans, and other essentials can mean starvation for some, and the poorest almost always pay the highest price.

As mentioned at the beginning of this book, complex decisions are difficult even when starting with correct information; but when the assumptions are wrong or incomplete to begin with, bad decisions are likely to follow. We all lose when we make changes without considering the facts.

Do Your Homework

In June 2008 the media narrative focused on a story about an exciting horse named "Big Brown" running the Belmont Stakes. All the money and discussion was about this unbeatable horse. "Big Brown" came in last. The winner was a barely mentioned horse that. like "Big Brown," had never lost a race. It was bred from a line of 5 winners of the Belmont Stakes. Its trainer has a long record of winning at that track. But the narrative in the media was only about "Big Brown". A little homework examining the alternatives would have paid 38 to 1. Americans all need to do the homework and examine the alternatives that are outside the media narrative.

As we listen to all the political candidates promising "change" during this election season, we ought to be very careful. We need to ask, "What kind of changes do you have in mind?" It's easy to pick an idea that offers easy answers to complex problems; but many of our most serious problems exist because there are no easy answers.

Every change has a cost of some kind. Just as ethanol has proved to have a much higher cost to the world than the $10 billion subsidy the U.S. government is paying, we may find that many of the other changes now being proposed have hidden costs that we're not willing to pay. And if this great country loses sight of what it has, it risks making changes for which the costs can never equal the consequences.

Epilogue

As mentioned earlier, we couldn't cover every broad misconception in this book, but here are a few more examples of myths that seem to be unusually ubiquitous.

KYOTO AND GLOBAL EMISSIONS

The world-wide excoriation of George Bush for rejecting the Kyoto protocol was extraordinary. There are literally hundreds of thousands of web pages that mention, usually derisively, that George Bush refused to sign or "abandoned" the treaty. Even among those who have a vague idea that the proposed treaty to reduce global greenhouse emissions was flawed, most have the impression that it was simply tough-minded realism that caused Bush to reject it and take the hit. What few people know is that before Bush took office, the U.S. Senate voted 97-0 to reject the protocol. It didn't get one vote on either side of the aisle.

Step forward a decade. The United States is still widely criticized for being one of only two countries in the world that has not ratified the Kyoto treaty. It is less popular to point out that, with a few exceptions, the major countries that committed to reducing carbon emissions under the agreement are not doing it. Their carbon emissions are going up, not down, let alone declining enough to meet the ambitious goals of Kyoto. The noteworthy exceptions are Germany, which is benefiting from reduced emissions in the smokestack-filled former East Germany as it is rebuilt, and the small, homogeneous nations of Denmark and Norway.[1]

It may come as an even greater surprise that during the latest six years for which information is available (2000–2005), carbon emissions grew by 1.5% in the U.S., compared with 3.3% in the European Union. This is the Europe whose commitments to reduce emissions are often held up as an example, which has an elaborate carbon cap and trade system, and where the most vocal criticisms of American emissions policies come from. Greenhouse emissions, a broader measure than carbon emissions, were up .6% in the U.S. and .8% in the E.U. during the same time period.[2] Preliminary information indicates that 2006 emissions were down −1.8% in the U.S.[3] while estimates for Europe range from −.8% to +1%.[456] The U.S.'s favorable comparison was achieved in spite of faster economic growth, meaning its "greenhouse gas intensity"—a fair measure of progress—declined by significantly more than in the E.U.[7] Some of this was apparently due to weather conditions, but much was also driven by little publicized programs that followed George Bush's public commitment in the proposed 2002 Clear Skies Act to reduce carbon intensity in the U.S. by 18% in ten years. This proposal was blocked by Democrats in Congress because it replaced some outdated and unachievable goals in prior legislation with more realistic ones. The Administration therefore pressed forward to implement some of its measures administratively through the Environmental Protection Agency, by strongly encouraging the adoption of cleaner technologies in about 30 specific emissions-intensive industries through tax incentives, voluntary partnerships, streamlined processes, and mandates. The U.S. government increased its spending on natural resources and the environment by 41% over seven years[8] and committed more than $30 billion to climate science, technology, international assistance on emissions, and incentive programs.[9]

Later, in 2005, the U.S. forged an agreement with six Asian countries which is designed to complement Kyoto by encouraging and assisting in the adoption of new technologies that reduce emissions, especially in the use of coal. This agreement was later joined by Canada, as it became clearer that its own Kyoto commitments could not be met, and that the treaty itself was turning out to be less successful than hoped.

Much more could be written about U.S. progress, some of which is truly impressive, in reducing other forms of pollutants and acid rain by amounts of 48% to 98% over the past 30 years. The U.S. is well ahead of most regions of the world in reducing many or most of these forms of pollution. A lot of work has also been done in recent years to improve the health of our forests, national parks, farmlands, marine ecosystems, wetlands, water, and to clean up abandoned old industrial sites called "brownfields." Details of the Clear Skies Initiative, the Global Climate Change Initiative, the Asia-Pacific Partnership on Clean Development and Climate, and other programs can be found using Google. Unfortunately you'll have to wade through much criticism about how the proposals are just sell-outs with relaxed standards and too "industry-friendly" to find those showing that the actual results of these programs are beating those of the Kyoto protocol. You'll also have to brook the many thousands of snide comments about Bush's rejection of Kyoto.

"SCOOTER LIBBY JUSTICE"

Most people have heard that Scooter Libby, the high ranking advisor to Dick Cheney, was convicted of something—who knows what—related to "outing" CIA agent Valerie Plame. Not so many know that (a) it was not Scooter Libby that outed Valerie Plame, it was Richard Armitage, (b) the courts determined that Richard Armitage did not break any laws in doing so, and (c) it was already known when the special prosecutor took the case forward to court that Scooter Libby had not, in fact, outed anyone. What got Mr. Libby in trouble is that he told the prosecutor during the lengthy pre-trial questioning—fifteen months after the event in question—that he had learned Plame's identity from journalist Tim Russert when in fact he had actually learned it from his boss, Dick Cheney. Thus he was charged with perjury and obstruction of justice. But Dick Cheney was completely within his rights to have given that information to Mr. Libby, so there was neither an underlying crime committed nor any reason for a cover-up. Most of the one-sided coverage of Scooter Libby was clearly designed to portray—for effect, as explained in the introduction of this book—that his misdeed was something entirely different from, and more diabolical than, what was really the case, even assuming the worst.

A thoughtful analysis of Scooter Libby's conviction, including a letter from former New York Mayor Ed Koch explaining why he thinks Mr. Libby was falsely convicted, can be found at www.scooterlibby.org. Mayor Koch's courageous letter ends with a response to those he predicted would criticize him: "Many of those people believe, as I do, that the jury that found O.J. Simpson not guilty was wrong and have no problem in questioning the verdict of that jury."

HALIBURTON

Somewhere along the way during the past six years just the mention of Dick Cheney's name became a pejorative, and Halliburton, the company he used to lead, somehow became a dirty word. We're not sure, precisely, what the supposed accusations related to Halliburton actually were, but perhaps there were misconceptions being passed around the blogs. Vice President Cheney relinquished all of his stock in Halliburton when he was elected, and it was a good thing he did, because the stock tanked, dropping from a price of $18 a share when he was elected to $6.40 in September 2002. As of mid-2005 it was only up to $21 a share, a small increase considering the market was booming. So, if there was some conspiratorial government assistance being directed toward Halliburton, (a) Cheney would not have benefited from it, and (b) it wasn't very effective.

Halliburton's stock began climbing again in 2007 as it became obvious that there would be a surge in the need for the company's oil drilling services. In fact, those services were needed five years earlier far more than some in our government realized, and not putting them to work more broadly led to the current oil shortage. Chalk one up— a costly one for Americans—for misconceptions leading to misguided decisions.

We believe we've shown a predictable pattern of beliefs about America—usually negative ones—that are widely held but not correct. Similar correctives could be written about negative narratives on "stolen elections," "wiretapping," "torture," stem cell research, Alberto Gonzales, No Child Left Behind, and many other controversial subjects. The net of it all is that much of the negativity about America is either overblown for effect or just wrong. America is still great and getting better. While no figures on the subject seem to be available, we suspect that despite its faults, America's press and news coverage is probably also the best in the world. As with all things though, there are good elements and bad ones, and there have been good times as well as times of turmoil. When the pace of transformation in the media settles down a bit, those outlets most committed to journalistic integrity will be well rewarded with success. America stands for things. It stands for doing what it has committed it will do—think Iraq, Afghanistan, Katrina, Social Security, nuclear challenges, and even Kyoto, where the commitments made by all have proven impossible to meet. America also stands for truth. We should all do our part to make sure that the commitment to this sure and steady principle that underpinned America's rise to greatness remains strong.

As a reminder, you can go to www.realitycheck-us.com to comment and get updated information.

Afterward

How Polls Can Mislead

In the introduction we stressed the increased importance of critical thinking and doing your homework in the new chaotic world of information overload and bias. We suggested asking the question: "compared to what" when you see information suggesting a trend is either good or bad.

Critical thinking also requires an understanding of how opinion polls can and often do mislead through non-neutral language, and by sequencing questions in a way that leads to a particular answer. Any complex and controversial issue has pros and cons that must be weighed. If the pollster simply lines up questions that point out all the pros in advance of the key question, respondents naturally feel they should be consistent with the answers they've just given. If all the cons were pointed out first, the outcome will be different.

Let's take a look at how this might work:

Approach A

1. Would you say that terrorist groups like al 'Qaeda, who answer to no government and want to destroy civil societies, pose a risk

to Americans? (No risk at all   Very little risk   Some risk   Significant risk ☐   Very serious risk ☐)

2. Do you think it is likely al 'Qaeda will try and carry out another attack like 9/11? (No chance at all ☐   Very little chance ☐   Some chance ☐   Likely ☐   Highly Likely ☐)

3. The Geneva Convention outlines standards for treating enemy prisoners who have followed certain rules such as wearing uniforms while in battle. Do you agree Al 'Qaeda combatants captured in battle should be entitled the same rights as those who have followed the Geneva Convention rules? Strongly disagree ☐   Disagree ☐   Neither Agree nor Disagree ☐   Agree ☐   Strongly Agree ☐

4. Do you agree that al 'Qaeda prisoners captured on the battlefield should have the same rights to a taxpayer funded trial as American citizens, or is a military trial sufficient? (Strongly disagree ☐   Disagree ☐   Neither Agree nor Disagree ☐   Agree ☐   Strongly Agree ☐)

Headline: "Poll indicates 85% of Americans disagree with Supreme Court ruling giving enemy combatants right to trial."

Approach B

1. Do you think it is right to keep someone in jail for years without any chance to argue his innocence?

2. Do you agree that denying al 'Qaeda prisoners in Guantanamo the right to a civilian trial fuels anti-American hatred around the world?

3. Do you agree that anti-American hatred puts the country at greater risk?

4. Do you agree that the U.S. should stand as a high example of the rule of law and apply it even when it is not expedient?

5. Do you agree al 'Qaeda prisoners captured on the battlefield should have the same rights to a taxpayer funded trial as American citizens?

Headline: "Poll indicates 78% agree with Supreme Court ruling granting right to American trial for al 'Qaeda combatants."

For polls to be valid and useful, great pains must be taken to ensure neutral language and objective question sequencing. The necessary rigor is often not taken by organizations whose objective is to sell news or a particular narrative to their audience of choice.

Endnotes

Introduction

1. May 2004 Pew Research Study, in conjunction with the Project for Excellence in Journalism and the Committee of Concerned Journalists.
2. "Partners and Adversaries: The Contentious Connection Between Congress and the Media." Among 139 Washington-based bureau chiefs and congressional correspondents who completed their questionnaire, 89% had voted for Bill Clinton in 1992, while just 7% had voted for George Bush.
3. "Even Harvard Finds the Media Biased," *Investory's Business Daily*, Nov. 1, 2007 [http://www.ibdeditorials.com/IBDArticles.aspx?id=278808786575124] (accessed Apr. 14, 2008).2007, Harvard's Shorenstein Center on the Press, Politics and Public Policy in conjunction with the Politics and Public Policy in conjunction with the Project for Excellence in Journalism, part of the Pew Research Center for People and the Press.
4. Ibid.

Chapter One

1. For example, if something grows +2 units from 100 to 102, this represents an increase of +2%. If something grows from 10 units to +2, the same growth of +2 represents a +20% increase. The U.S. starts from a base that is already many times the size of most of the other economies

on this list, so a small percentage growth actually represents a massive increase in actual wealth.

2. Source: CIA World Factbook.

Chapter 2

1. Source: http://www.irs.gov/taxstats/indtaxstats/article/0,,id=96679,00.html

Chapter 3

1. Helen Murphy, Christopher Swann and Mark Drajem, "China's Power Erodes Free-Trade Support in Developing Nations," Bloomberg.com, April 2, 2007. [http://www.bloomberg.com/apps/news?pid=20601087&sid=ar_m7AGPgNlA&refer=home] (accessed April 2, 2007).

2. Editorial, "Pursuing Sustainable Growth," *China Daily*, Mar. 30, 2004. [http://www.china.org.cn/english/China/91699.htm] (accessed Apr. 3, 2008).

3. Joseph Kahn and Jim Yardley, "As China Roars, Pollution Reaches Deadly Extremes," *New York Times*, Aug. 26,2007. [http://www.nytimes.com/2007/08/26/world/asia/26china.html] (accessed May 10, 2008).

4. "China says water pollution so severe that cities could lack safe supplies," *China Daily*, Jun. 7, 2005. [http://www.chinadaily.com.cn/english/doc/2005–06/07/content_449451.htm] (accessed May 10, 2008).

5. Keith Bradsher and David Barboza, "Pollution from Chinese Coal Casts a Global Shadow," *New York Times*, June 11, 2006. [www.nytimes.com/2006/06/11/business.worldbusiness/11chinacoal.html] (accessed May 10, 2008).

6. Joe Macdonald, AP, *op cit.*

7. G. Marland, T.A. Boden, R.J. Andres. "Global, Regional, and National CO_2 Emissions," in *Trends: A Compendium of Data on Global Change (2007)."* Carbon Dioxide Information Analysis Center, Oak Ridge National Laboratory, U.S. Department of Energy, Oak Ridge, Tennessee. Available at: http://cdiac.ornl.gov/trends/emis/tre_usa.htm. (Accessed May 12, 2008).

8. Joe McDonald, "China's Inflation Rises to Almost 12-year High," *Associated Press,* May 12,2008. [http://license.icopyright.net/user/viewfreeuse.act?fuid=MTAOTczNw%3D%3D] (accessed May 12, 2008).

Chapter 4

1. Source: *The Economist,* "2008 Pocket World in Figures"

Chapter 5

1. John C. McCarthy, "Near-Term Growth of Offshoring Accelerating," *Forrester Research,* May 14, 2004. [http://www.forrester.com/Research/Document/Excerpt/0,7211,34426,00.html] (accessed Apr. 3, 2008).

2. Bruce Nussbaum, "Special Report: Where Are the Jobs?" *BusinessWeek,* Mar. 22, 2004. [http://www.businessweek.com/magazine/content/04_12/b3875601.htm] (accessed Apr. 3, 2008).

3. "How Can the Federal Government Help?" Hon. Sherwood L. Boehlert, Chairman, Hearing before the subcommittee on environment, technology, and standards, U.S. House of Representatives Committee on Science and Technology. Document 87–544PS, June 5, 2003 http://commdocs.house.gov/committees/science/hsy87544.000/hsy87544_0f.htm

4. The complaint during the recent recovery, that it was a jobless recovery, was due largely to the fact that the U.S. was not adding jobs as fast as in previous recoveries. Jobs were being added and the unemployment rate was dropping, but Non Farm Payroll statistics weren't jumping by the hundreds of thousands per month, as they had in previous recoveries. The reason for this is two-fold. First, unemployment did not get as high in 2002 as in previous recessions, so there was less of a gap to fill as the recovery developed. Second, productivity was increasing quickly. American factories and mines were able to grow rapidly without adding employees to the same degree as previous recoveries, because worker productivity was increasing. This is another way of saying the workers were becoming more valuable, and in the long run this leads to higher pay.

5. See: www.federalreserve.gov/FOMC/BeigeBook/2008/

Chapter 6

1. U.S. Department of Labor—The Labor Advocate—https://www.youth2work.gov/_sec/laboradvocate.

2. ditto

3. US Dept of Labor—Bureau of Labor Statistics—Tables B-3 and 1—April 2008 vs April 2001. Note, this is not inflation adjusted like the figure immediately above it.

4. Thomas Sowell, *Economic Facts and Fallacies*, p. 125.

5. Ibid. p. 130.

6. U.S. Census Bureau, "Income, Poverty, and Health Insurance Coverage in the United States: 2006 Report, Aug. 28, 2007. [http://www.census.gov/prod/2007pubs/p60-233.pdf] (accessed Apr. 4, 2008).

8. Subir Lall, Florence Jaumotte, Chris Papageorgiou, and Petia Topalova, "Globalization and Inequality," in *World Economic Outlook*. Washington, DC: International Monetary Fund, October 2007. 31*ff*.

9. Gerald E. Auten and Geoffrey Gee, "Income Mobility in the U.S.: Evidence from Income Tax Returns for 1987 and 1996." Washington, DC: U.S. Department of the Treasury: OTA Paper #99, May 2007. [http://www.treas.gov/offices/tax-policy/library/ota99.pdf] (accessed Apr. 4, 2008).

10. U.S. Bureau of the Census: Wilfred T. Masumura, "Moving Up and Down the Income Ladder," The Dynamics of Person Well-Being: Report No. P70-65, July 1998. [http://www.census.gov/prod/2/pop/p70/p70-56.pdf] (accessed Apr. 4, 2008).

11. Lawrence Mishel, Jared Bernstein, and John Schmitt, *State of Working America: 2000–01* (Ithaca, NY: Cornell University Press, 2000), p. 77.

Chapter 7

1. For more on this, see the World Economic Outlook data at the International Monetary Fund (IMF) at http://www.imf.org/external/pubs/ft/weo/2008/01/weodata/weoselgr.aspx.

2. The term "trade weighted" refers to an index calculated by the Board of Governors of the U.S. Federal Reserve system that weighs each currency against the dollar, based on the total volume of trade that each country has with the United States.

3. These data from the IMF, except for Foreign Exchange Rate information from the Bloomberg News Service.

4. These data from the IMF.

Chapter 8

1. Suzann Chapman, "The War Before the War," *Air Force Magazine*: Vol. 87, No. 2, Feb. 2004. [http://www.afa.org/magazine/Feb2004/0204war.asp]

(accessed May 20, 2008). See also: David Usborne, "The West's Forgotten Conflict: US & UK Have Flown 280,000 'Sorties' Bombing Iraqis," *The Independent*, June 23, 2000. [Available at: http://commondreams.org/views/062300-102.htm] (accessed May 10, 2008).

2. Hassan Hafidh, "Iraq Says Civilians Killed," *The Washington Post*, Sepember 11, 2001. and Julian Borger, "Democrats lash Bush 'lunacy' on missiles," *The Guardian*, Tuesday Sept. 11, 2001 http://www.guardian.co.uk/world/2001/sep/11/usa.julianborger1

3. Stephen Zunes, "The United States and the Kurds: A Brief History," *Foreign Policy in Focus*, Oct. 25, 2007. [http://www.fpif.org/fpiftxt/4670] (accessed May 10, 2008). See also: Carl Rochelle, "U.S. readies forces in response to Iraqi attack on Kurds," *CNN Interactive* (inlcues AP and Reuters reports), Aug. 31, 1996. [http://www.cnn.com/WORLD/9608/31/iraq.forces/] (accessed May 10, 2008).

4. The text of United Nations Security Council Resolution 1441 is available at: http://www.worldpress.org/specials/iraq/unscr1441.htm. The text of Security Council Resolution 686, affirming the continued relevance of the twelve previous resolutions demanding Iraqi compliance is available at: http://www.worldpress.org/specials/iraq/unscr686.htmresolutions, but Resolution 686

5. News of the U.N. decision to demand compliance and President Bush's final offer of a peaceful settlement to Saddam Hussein were broadcast on both sides of the Atlantic. Transcript of the President's national address, "Bush: 'Leave Iraq within 48 hours,'" *CNN*, Mar. 17, 2003. [http://www.cnn.com/2003/WORLD/meast/03/17/sprj.irq.bush.transcript/]. See also: "Bush sets deadline on Iraq," *BBC*, Mar. 17, 2003. [http://news.bbc.co.uk/2/hi/middle_east/2855461.stm]

6. The complete text of Resolution 1441 with precedents and documentation, is available in PDF format at the United Nations website: www.un.org/depts/unmovic/documents/1441.pdf.

7. A partial list of the WMD that went missing from Saddam's stockpiles, according to official U.N. reports, included: 3.9 tons of VX nerve agent, 6,526 aerial chemical bombs, 550 mustard gas shells, 2,062 tons of mustard precursors, 15,000 chemical munitions, 8,445 liters of Anthrax, 11,000 liters of botulinum toxin, as well as SCUD missiles and rockets armed with chemicals. Inspectors of the Iraq Study Group have suggested that these and other munitiions were transferred illegally to underground storage sites in Syria, Jordan, and Iran prior to the U.S.-led invasion in March 2003.

8. See for example: Brian Kraiker, "A Tyrant's Life," *Newsweek*, Dec. 14, 2006. [http://216.109.125.130/search/cache?ei=UTF-8&p=WMD+% 228%2C000+Kurds%22&fr=yfp-t-501&u=] (accessed Apr. 9, 2008). A detailed report on the Anfal massacre can be found on the Internet: Andrew Whitley, George Black, et al., "Genocide in Iraq: The Anfal Campaign Against the Kurds." a Special Report. New York: Human Rights Watch, 1993. [http://hrw.org/reports/1993/iraqanfal/] (accessed Apr. 9, 2008).

9. For those with the courage and a strong stomach, a heartrending Youtube video on the Anfal massacre and memorial is available, powerful even in Kurdish, at: http://www.youtube.com/watch?v=dBX2_byWYgc.

10. The military coalition included Argentina, Australia, Bahrain, Bangladesh, Belgium, Canada, Czechoslovakia, Denmark, Egypt, France, Greece, Hungary, Italy, Kuwait, Morocco, the Netherlands, New Zealand, Niger, Norway, Oman, Pakistan, Poland, Qatar, Saudi Arabia, Senegal, South Korea, Spain, Syria, the United Arab Emirates, the United Kingdom, and the United States.

11 "Oil-for-Food Facts" provides a general overview of the subject at www.oil forfoodfacts.org/history.aspx.

12. Susan Schmidt, "Plame's Input Is Cited on Niger Mission: Report Disputes Wilson's Claims on Trip, Wife's Role," *Washington Post*, July 10, 2004. [http://www.washingtonpost.com/wp-dyn/articles/A39834-2004Jul9.html] (accessed July 11, 2007). For a better view of the animus in this case, an excellent analysis may be found in the book by *Washington Examiner* reporter Rowan Scarborough, *Sabotage: America's Enemies within the CIA*. Washington, DC: Regnery, 2007.

13. "Bill Clinton on Bush uranium line: 'Everybody makes mistakes': Former president accepts explanation on State of the Union," CNN.com, July 23, 2003. [http://www.cnn.com/2003/ALLPOLITICS/07/23/clinton.iraq.sotu/] (accessed Apr. 1, 2008).

14. U.S. News and World Report, May 19, 2008, Rethinking the Iraq Critics, by Michael Barone,

15. Ibid.

16. For those interested in more details on the production and concealment of WMD in Syria, check out these websites: http://www.2la.org/syria/ wmd.html, and http://www.2la.org/syria/iraq-wmd.php.

17. General Georges Sada, *Saddam's Secrets: How an Iraqi General Defied and Survived Saddam Hussein*. Nashville: Integrity, 2006. A review and

discussion of the generals' testimony and the book can be found at http://www.cnsnews.com/ViewSpecialReports.asp?Page=/SpecialReports/archive/200602/SPE20060202a.html.

18. Ed Finn, "Grand Ayatollah Sayyid Ali Husaini Sistani: Why we'd better listen to Iraq's influential cleric," Slate.com, Feb. 4, 2004. [http://www.slate.com/id/2094814/0 (accessed Apr. 3, 2008).

19. Kenneth M. Pollack, "Five Ways to Win Back Iraq," *New York Times*, July 1, 2005. [http://www.nytimes.com/2005/07/01/opinion/01pollack.html] (accessed Apr. 7, 2008).

20. Mohammed Daraghmeh, "Saddam Hussein raises reward Iraq will pay for suicide bombings," *The Associated Press*, April 3, 2002.

21. Trudy Rubin, "Northern Iraq is a region on edge," *Knight Ridder Newspapers*, Feb 25, 2003 http://www.accessmylibrary.com/coms2/summary_0286-6034109_ITM

22. CNN, "Iraqi Council Member: Saddam hid $40 billion," Tuesday, December 30, 2003.

23. Con Coughlin, "Saddam's WMD hidden in Syria, says Iraq survey chief," *London Daily Telegraph*, Jan. 24, 2004. [http://www.telegraph.co.uk/news/main.jhtml?xml=/news/2004/01/25/wirq25.xml&sSheet=/news/2004/01/25/ixnewstop.html] (accessed Nov. 12, 2005).

24. "Ex-agent says U.S. ignored WMD sites: Waged 3-year battle to conduct searches, but politics, fear got in way," WorldNetDaily.com, Aug. 5, 2006. [http://www.worldnetdaily.com/news/article.asp?ARTICLE_ID=51394] (accessed Nov. 11, 2006).

25. An eye-opening interview with Mr. Tierney can be found at: Jamie Glazov, "Where the WMDs Went: An Interview with Bill Tierney," *FrontPage magazine*, Nov. 16, 2005. [http://www.frontpagemag.com/Articles/Read.aspx?GUID=D47C7304-B454-4294-8A21-DBEC5E2AACBE] (accessed Nov. 30, 2005).

26. Jim Geraghty, "The WMD Road to Damascus," *National Review*, Jan. 12, 2004. [http://article.nationalreview.com/?q=NmEwNzY3MjRiNzA4YTc1YTk0MWNiYzgxMjcwMDU3YTg=] (accessed Nov. 11, 2005).

27. Ira Stoll, "Saddam's WMD Moved to Syria, An Israeli Says," *New York Sun*, Dec. 15, 2005. [http://www2.nysun.com/article/24480] (accessed Mar. 8, 2007).

28. See Hayden Peake, The CIA Review of: Mahdi Obeidi and Kurt Pitzer, *The Bomb in My Garden: The Secrets of Saddam's Nuclear Mastermind.*

Hoboken, NJ: John Wiley & Sons, 2004. [https://www.cia.gov/library/center-for-the-study-of-intelligence/csi-publications/csi-studies/studies/vol48no4/bombs_in_garden.html] (accessed Aug. 30, 2005).

29. Iraqi General Georges Sada offers the following accounting of casualties in the book, *Saddam's Secrets*, cited above: "Of the approximately 360,000 Iraqi soldiers on the field of battle, 28% of them (or nearly 100,000 men and boys) were killed in action, and as many as 200,000 sustained serious injuries. In addition, coalition forces captured 60,000 prisoners, and by some estimates there may have been as many as 150,000 deserters. As for casualties on the other side, 390 American soldiers, sailors, and airmen died in combat, while 458 were wounded in action. Among coalition forces, there was a total of 510 casualties. The financial cost to America was approximately $80 billion, of which coalition nations contributed $54 billion. In the end, it's clear that Saddam had underestimated the resolve of the American forces, and he completely misjudged the unity and determination of the coalition." (*Saddam's Secrets*, pp. 189–190).

30. "Major Military Operation since World War II," Ask the Editors: Fact Monster. Pearson Education online. [http://www.factmonster.com/timelines/militaryoperations.html] (accessed Apr. 9, 2008).

31. L. Paul Bremer with Malcolm McConnell. *My Year in Iraq: The Struggle to Build a Future of Hope*. New York: Simon & Schuster, 2006.

Chapter 9

1. "Afghanistan: UN will stay as long as it takes to ensure peace," *Adnkronos* (Italy: Published online in English), Apr. 4, 2008. [http://www.adnkronos.com/AKI/English/Security/?id=1.0.2038926041] (accessed Apr. 9, 2008).

2. "NATO making a difference in Afghanistan," *Pak Tribune* (Pakistan News Service), Nov. 12, 2006. [http://www.paktribune.com/news/index.shtml?159681] (accessed Mar. 30, 2008).

Chapter 10

1. Energy Information Administration, "Short Term Energy Outlook," May 2008.

2. Energy Information Administration, "Oil Market Report," April 11, 2008.

3. Jad Mouawad and Julia Werdigier, "Warning on Impact of China and India Oil Demand," *New York Times*, Nov. 7, 2007. [http://www.nytimes.com/2007/11/07/business/07cnd-energy.html?ex=1352091600&en=62d1adc06b1f0d1b&ei=5088&partner=rssnyt&emc=rss] (accessed Apr. 8, 2008).

4. Matthew Forney, :China's Quest for Oil," *Time* magazine, Oct. 18, 2004. [http://www.time.com/time/magazine/article/0,9171,501041025-725174,00.html] (accessed Apr. 8, 2008).

5. Ibid.

6. Chris Baldwin, "You think we've got it bad? Gas prices kick world motorists," *Reuters*, Apr. 19, 2007. [http://www.usatoday.com/money/industries/energy/2007-04-19-world-gas_N.htm] (accessed Apr. 8, 2008).

7. Steve Hargreaves, "How much Exxon pays for oil," CNNMoney.com, Nov. 6 2007. [http://money.cnn.com/2007/11/05/news/companies/exxon_oil/index.htm?postversion=2007110613] (accessed Apr. 10, 2008).

8. Ibid.

9. J. Perry, "Exxon's 2007 Tax Bill: $30 Billion," *Seeking Alpha* (Investment Analysis), Feb. 5, 2008. [http://seekingalpha.com/article/63131-exxon-s-2007-tax-bill-30-billion?source=side_bar_editors_picks] (accessed Apr. 8, 2007).

10. Walter E. Williams, "Big Corn and Ethanol Hoax," *Human Events*, Mar. 11, 2008. [http://www.humanevents.com/article.php?id=25437] (accessed Mar. 11, 2008).

11. Manuel Roig-Franzia, "A Culinary and Cultural Staple in Crisis: Mexico Grapples With Soaring Prices for Corn—and Tortillas," *Washington Post*, Jan. 27, 2007. A1.

12. Editorial: "Corn-based ethanol not cheap, not green," *The Economist*, reprinted in the Seattle Post-Intelligencer, Apr. 11, 2007. [http://seattlepi.nwsource.com/opinion/311225_ethanol12.html] (accessed Apr. 8, 2008). See Also: John Roach, "Ethanol Not So Green After All?" *National Geographic News*, July 11, 2006. [http://news.nationalgeographic.com/news/2006/07/060711-ethanol-gas.html] (accessed Apr. 8, 2008).

13. Michael Grunwald, "The Clean Energy Scam," *Time* magazine, Apr. 7, 2008. 40–45.

14. Salvatore Lazzari, "The Windfall Profit Tax On Crude Oil: Overview of The Issues," Congressional Research Service, Sept. 12, 1990. [http://www.taxfoundation.org/files/110805crs_windfall.pdf] (accessed Apr. 8, 2008).

15. Marlo Lewis, Jr., "A Windfall of Bad Ideas," Competitive Enterprise Institute, Dec. 4, 2005. [http://cei.org/gencon/019,05026.cfm] (accessed Apr. 8, 2008).

16. H. Sterling Burnett and Christa Bieker, "Taxing Profits, Draining Energy," National Center for Policy Analysis, Brief Analysis No. 549, March 30, 2006. [http://www.ncpa.org/pub/ba/ba549/] (accessed Apr. 8, 2008).

Chapter 11

1. United Nations: Office of the Iraq Programme, Oil-for-Food: http://www.un.org/Depts/oip/

2. Anne Penketh, "Anti-war nations 'took bribes' before war began," *The Independent* (UK), Jan. 28, 2004. [http://www.independent.co.uk/news/world/middle-east/antiwar-nations-took-bribes-before-war-began-574699.html] (accessed Nov. 20, 2006).

3. *New York Times,* 1986.

4. Therese Raphael, "The Oil-for-Food Scandal," *Wall Street Journal,* Mar. 11, 2004. [http://online.wsj.com/article/SB107896733191552156.html] (accessed Nov. 7, 2006).

Chapter 12

1. "The Treaty on the Non-Proliferation of Nuclear Weapons" (NPT), United Nations. Full text available at http://www.un.org/events/npt2005/npttreaty.html] (accessed May 10, 2008).

2. Countries currently engaged in supporting U.S. effort in Iraq include Afghanistan, Albania, Angola, Australia, Azerbaijan, Bulgaria, Colombia, Czech Republic, Denmark, Dominican, Republic, El Salvador, Eritrea, Estonia, Ethiopia, Georgia, Honduras, Hungary, Iceland, Italy, Japan, Kuwait, Latvia, Lithuania, Macedonia, Marshall Islands, Micronesia, Mongolia, Netherlands, Nicaragua, Palau, Panama, Philippines, Poland, Portugal, Romania, Rwanda, Singapore, Slovakia, Solomon Islands, South Korea, Spain, Tonga, Turkey, Uganda, Ukraine, the United Kingdom, the United States, and Uzbekistan, and the number is still growing. The list includes nations from every continent. Population of coalition countries totals more than 1.23 billion people, with a combined GDP of approximately $22 trillion and represents every major race, religion, and ethnicity. It should come

as no surprise that many of these countries have recently overthrown repressive regimes or have suffered from terrorist activities. These 49 nations understand the threat that Saddam Hussein posed to the world and the devastation his regime inflicted on their own people.

3. Los Angeles Times staff writers, U.S. offers evidence of North Korea-Syria nuclear plant, April 25, 2008

4. David Albright and Paul Brannan, "Syria Update III: New information about Al Kibar reactor site," Institute for Science and International Security, Apr. 24, 2008. [http://www.isis-online.org/publications/syria/SyriaUpdate_24April2008.pdf] (accessed May 5, 2008).

5. Editorial: "Translating the Iran NIE," *The Economist*, Mar. 20, 2008. [http://www.economist.com/blogs/democracyinamerica/iran/] (accessed Apr. 9, 2008).

6. Rasmussen Reports: "Just 18% Believe Iran has Stopped Nuclear Weapons Development Program," Dec. 7, 2007. [http://www.rasmussenreports.com/public_content/politics/current_events/general_current_events/just_18_believe_iran_has_stopped_nuclear_weapons_development_program] (accessed Apr. 8, 2008).

7. Rowan Scarborough, "Intelligence officials downplay Iran report," *Washington Times*, Apr. 4, 2008. [http://www.washingtontimes.com/article/20080404/nation/866512695] (accessed Apr. 9, 2008).

8. Michael Hirsh, Melinda Liu, and George Wehrfritz, "We Are a Nuclear Power," *Newsweek*, Oct. 23, 2006. [http://www.newsweek.com/id/44943] (accessed Apr. 10, 2008).

9. Kim Holmes, "Iran: Don't Trust an Abuser with Nukes," *Heritage* Web-Memo #824, Aug. 26, 2005. [http://www.heritage.org/Research/Iran/wm824.cfm] (accessed Apr. 10, 2008).

10. Levite, Ariel E. "Never Say Never Again: Nuclear Reversal Revisited." *International Security*, vol. 27, no. 3: Winter 2002. 59–88.

11. Robert Samuelson, "Nuclear Nightmare," *Washington Post*, Oct. 20, 2004. A27.

Chapter 13

1. Charles Taylor and Dan Miller, "Gulf Coast Still Recovering Six Months After Katrina," National Association of Counties, Mar. 10, 2006. [http://www.naco.org/Template.cfm?Section=Publications&template=/ContentManagement/ContentDisplay.cfm&ContentID=19222] (accessed Apr. 12, 2008).

2. Douglas Brinkley, *The Great Deluge: Hurricane Katrina, New Orleans, and the Mississippi Gulf Coast.* New York: Morrow, 2006. 416.

3. Brinkley, 229.

5. To understand the lengths that authors of one-sided books about Katrina, all of which were bent on pinning the majority of blame for anything that went wrong during Katrina on FEMA and the Bush administration, here are a few illustrative anecdotes, One claimed that the buses might not have started. To point out the obvious, this was the city's official school bus transportation system. If they worked well enough to take children to school five days a week, one would think they would work just as well in an evacuation. Other criticisms of FEMA included the charge that they hadn't developed a detailed evacuation plan. How hard could that have been? "You're in charge of getting drivers. You're in charge of identifying fifteen pick-up points on a map. You're in charge of making copies of the maps. You're in charge of making signs and placing them around the city." Fortunately, local Wildlife and Fisheries oficers didn't wait for the city or anyone else to come up with a plan. They simply reacted.

6. Thevenot, Brian; Russell, Gordon. "Reports of anarchy at Superdome overstated." *Seattle Times,* September 26, 2005.

7. *The Great Deluge,* by Douglas Brinkley

8. Bipartisan report on Katrina.

Chapter 14

1. Richard Wolf, "Social Security Hits First Wave of Boomers," *USA Today,* Oct. 8, 2007. [http://www.usatoday.com/news/washington/2007-10-08-boomers_N.htm] (accessed Apr. 12, 2008).

2. Richard Morin and Dale Russakoff, "Social Security Problems Not a Crisis, Most Say," *Washington Post,* Feb. 10, 2005. A1.

3. Laura D'andrea Tyson, "Social Security Crisis? What Crisis?" *Business-Week,* Jan. 17, 2005. [http://www.businessweek.com/magazine/content/05_03/b3916024_mz007.htm] (accessed Apr. 12, 2008).

4. Eric Bates, "The Fake Crisis," *Rolling Stone,* Jan. 13, 2005. [http://www.rolling stone.com/politics/story/6822964/the_fake_crisis/] (accessed Apr. 12, 2008).

5. John R. Gist, "Population Aging, Entitlement Growth, and the Economy," AARP Public Policy Institute, Jan. 2007. [http://www.aarp.org/research/assistance/entitlement/inb135_security.html] (accessed Apr. 12, 2008).

Chapter 15

1. Data from U.S. Census Bureau, available at http://www.census.gov/hhes/www/housing/hvs/qtrl108.

2. Rick Brooks and Constance Mitchell Ford, "The United States of Subprime: Data Show Bad Loans Permeate the Nation; Pain Could Last Years," *Wall Street Journal*, Oct. 11, 2007. [http://online.wsj.com/article/SB119205925519455321.html?mod=hpp_us_whats_news] (accessed Mar. 11, 2008).

3. David Henry and Matthew Goldstein, "The Bear Flu: How It Spread: A novel financing scheme used by Bear Stearns' hedge funds became a template for subprime disaster," *BusinessWeek*, Dec. 19, 2007. [http://www.businessweek.com/print/magazine/content/07_53/b4065000402886.htm] (accessed Apr. 18, 2008).

4. CitiFX Strategy Liquidity and Credit Crisis Monitor. April 29, 2008.

5. Commentary by Michael Cembalest, CIO of JP Morgan Private Bank, for "Eye on the Market," Apr. 30, 2008.

6. Anthony Downs, "Credit Crisis: The Sky is not Falling," Brookings Institution Policy Brief #164, May 11, 2007. [http://www.brookings.edu/papers/2007/10_mortgage_industry_downs.aspx] (accessed May 15, 2008).

7. Craig Guillot, "'Average' buyer can't afford home," BankRate.com via Yahoo! Finance, Apr. 17, 2008. [http://biz.yahoo.com/brn/080417/24868.html] (accessed May 10, 2008).

Chapter 16

1. John C. Goodman, "A Plan for Real Health Reform," Heartland Institute: *Health Care News*, May 1, 2008. [http://www.heartland.org/Article.cfm?artId=23041] (accessed Apr. 21, 2008).

2. Richard E. Ralston, "Private Health-Care Options Must Be Defended," For Health Freedom, July 24, 2007. [http://forhealthfreedom.org/Newsletter/July2007.html#Article2] (accessed Apr. 15, 2008).

3. March 18 Policy Analysis.

4. Break in series; see "Comparability over time" at http://www.irdes.fr/ecosante/OCDE/411.html.

5. Ezekiel J. Emanuel and Victor R. Fuchs, "Who really pays for health care?" *Chicago Tribune*, Mar. 27, 2008. [http://www.chicagotribune.com/news/chi-oped0327healthmar27,0,7118131.story] (accessed Apr. 21, 2008).

6. Gary Langer, "Health Care Pains: Growing Health Care Concerns Fuel Cautious Support for Change," *ABC News*, Oct. 20, 2003. [abcnews.go.com/ sections/living/US/healthcare031020_poll.html] (accessed Apr. 11, 2008).

7. "Poll Finds Americans Split by Political Party over Whether Socialized Medicine Better or Worse than Current System" Harvard School of Public Health, Feb. 14, 2008. [http://www.hsph.harvard.edu/news/press-releases/ 2008-releases/poll-americans-split-by-political-party-over-socialized-medicine.html] (accessed Apr. 12, 2008).

8. Christopher J. Conover, "Health Care Regulation: A $169 Billion Hidden Tax," Policy Analysis No. 527; Oct. 4, 2004. [http://www.cato.org/pubs/pas/ html/pa527/pa527index.html] (accessed Apr. 12, 2008).

9. Laura Donnelly and Patrick Sawer, "Record numbers go abroad for health," *London Sunday Telegraph*, Oct. 28, 2007. [http://www.telegraph.co .uk/global/main.jhtml?xml=/global/2007/10/28/noindex/nhealth128.xml] (Accessed Apr. 7, 2008)

10. Kevin A. Hassett, "Hillary and Health Care Prove a Toxic Mix Again," Bloomberg.com, Sept. 24, 2007. [http://www.aei.org/publications/filter.all, pubID.26850/pub_detail.asp] (accessed Apr. 20, 2008).

11. Ezekiel J. Emanuel and Victor R. Fuchs, *op cit.*

12. Richard E. Ralston, "Health Savings Accounts (HSAs) Ease Tax Burden," Americans for Free Choice in Medicine.

13. Malcolm Kline, "Academics Downgrade Socialized Medicine," Accuracy in Media, Mar. 25, 2008. [http://campusreportonline.net/main/articles.php? id=2238]: With reference to: [http://www.john-goodman-blog.com/five-fascinating-results/#more-184] (accessed Apr. 11, 2008).

14. Daniel P. Kessler, John F. Cogan, and Glenn Hubbard, "Healthy, Wealthy, and Wise," *Wall Street Journal*, May 4, 2004. [http://healthpolicy.stanford .edu/news/wall_street_journal_oped_advocates_freemarket_solution_for_ us_health_care_20040506/] (accessed Apr. 12, 2008).

15. John F. Cogan, "Bringing the Market to Health Care," *Wall Street Journal*, Sept. 15, 2007. [http://online.wsj.com/article/SB118982607519428545 .html] (accessed Apr. 18, 2008).

Chapter 17

1 Office of the U.S. Trade Representative, "Policy Brief: NAFTA Facts," Oct. 2007. [http://www.export.gov/fta/nafta/nafta_benefits.pdf] (accessed Apr. 15, 2008).

2. USDA: Foreign Agricultural Service. Backgrounder: "Benefits of NAFTA," May 2005. [http://www.fas.usda.gov/itp/policy/nafta/nafta_backgrounder.htm] (accessed Apr. 20, 2008).

3. "Debunking USTR Claims in Defense of NAFTA: The Real NAFTA Score 2008," PublicCitizen.org. 2007. [http://www.citizen.org/trade/nafta/articles.cfm?ID=17640] (accessed Mar. 21, 2008).

Epilogue

1. United Nations Framework Convention on Climate Change, Time Series—Annex 1 nations, http://unfccc.int/ghg_data/ghg_data_unfccc/time_series_annex_i/items/3844.php

2. United Nations Framework Convention on Climate Change, Time Series—Annex 1 nations http://unfccc.int/ghg_data/ghg_data_unfccc/time_series_annex_i/items/3842.php

3. "An Inconvenient Reduction," *The Wall Street Journal*, December 3, 2007

4. Drew Thornley, "Carbon Dioxide Emissions Fall in U.S., Rise in Europe," Environment & Climate News, March 1, 2008

5. Keith Johnson, "Carbon Copy: Europe's Still Not Cutting Emissions," The Wall Street Journal, April 2, 2008, 4:00 pm

6. Leigh Phillips, "EU remains off track to meet Kyoto targets," EU observer.com, June 19, 2008.

7. In the four years from 2000—2004, the U.S. greenhouse gas intensity dropped by 7.5% while the E.U. gas intensity dropped by about 4.5%. To illustrate the concept of energy intensity, if a country grows by 20% and emissions remain the same, clearly it has done more than a country whose emissions stay the same while there is no economic growth.

8. GPOaccess, Budget of the United States Government: Historical Tables Fiscal Year 2008, http://www.gpoaccess.gov/usbudget/fy08/sheets/hist03z2.xls

9. Kurt Volker—Remarks at the German Marshall Fund, "Post-Kyoto Surprise: America's Quiet Efforts to Cut Greenhouse Gases Are Producing Results," Berlin, Germany, February 12, 2007.

.